My So-Called Child Abuse, My Great Britain

CW00498296

By Joseph Kane

This book is dedicated to my Grandma, Marie, who loved and showed me the good side of life. Thanks gran x

This book is also dedicated to the thirty friends and family I have lost from murder, suicide, substance abuse, cancer, and natural causes. May God rest their soul, and may their spirits rest on my shoulders as I walk this earth alone until the end of my time in the name of Jesus Christ. Amen

"Tomorrow is a new day."

I would appreciate it if you left me a review on Amazon to help people find my book. Thanks

Table of Contents

Author's Notes

Please be aware that this book covers disturbing true stories that some readers may find upsetting. If you have experienced traumatic events in your life, I would advise that you don't read this book. Some of the stories consist of: Child abuse, animal abuse, sexual abuse, self-harm, attempted suicide, successful suicide, substance abuse, neglect, emotional abuse, poverty, violence, murder, mental illness, crime, homelessness, starvation, and cancer. This book is not a sweet lullaby. It will repulse and shock you to the core.

Some, but not all of the names have been changed in this book to respect the privacy of others. Out of respect for the dead, this story has been told exactly how it happened. My aim of this book is to share my story with the rest of the world so that others can learn from it. Some of you may be inspired to write your own life story. Being on this planet once, it's essential to take responsibility for our actions. I would also like to guide people who have experienced any physical, sexual or mental abuse. This book covers a wide range of social problems that can happen to a human being when certain conditions are met. Everything in this book is true, and none of the stories have been exaggerated. I wrote as it happened, how I felt and what I experienced – as God as my witness. Being blessed with a photographic memory, I have memories from a very young age.

I was born in 1985 in Preston, Lancashire, UK. My mum and dad, and their mum and dad lived at a time when there was a pub on every corner. It was the post-war decades where life had blossomed once again on the British Isles. If you were lucky to have great grandparents, then you are fortunate to exist. Not every soldier from World War 1 and 2 had the chance to procreate before their demise, even if they did make it to the end of the war. My great-grandfather survived the war but was gassed by the Germans, so he died in his sixties from lung disease/cancer. Because my grandparents were kids during the war or born around that time, they carried with them the British stiff upper lip. If you don't know what that means, it's fortitude and stoicism in the face of adversity, and exercises of great self-restraint in the expression of emotion. It basically means don't give a shit about anything. Americans love that about us for some reason. If only they saw the result. Thankfully now in 2019, we have services, medical pieces of evidence and advice to live a healthy and proactive life. My mum's dad owned a pub, and my dad was drinking and smoking in pubs from the age of fourteen so you can tell how this story is going to turn out when a child comes into the mix.

[Memory is] a man's real possession... In nothing else is he rich, in nothing else is he poor.

Alexander Smith (1830 – 1867)

Chapter 1 - Gate Crasher

It was Saturday, August the 10th 1985 when my grandma, along with other relatives had prepared the buffet for the party. My gran was like the head of the family. She was the one that got everyone together, arranged parties and made the buffets single-handed, that catered for over a hundred people. How she did it, I'll never know. It was my uncle's 21st birthday, so preparation for that night was in full swing. He was my dad's youngest brother, my dad being the oldest out of three lads. Everything came together like clockwork. The labour club function room was sitting in wait with hanging balloons and banners caped around. The barman in the corner eagerly awaited for the night ahead, locked and loaded with enough booze to kill a zoo. The DJ was finishing his set-up with a selection of 80's music, that unknowingly went down in history as some of the best music ever created. An army of ants had arrived with silver foil platters in each hand, full of sandwiches, savouries, and desserts. The birthday cake and whole stuffed salmon had to be carried with extra care. By the time it got to 6pm, everyone had arrived, and the party was going well with introductory drinks, warm welcomes, and laughs between tight-knit family and friends; nobody was a stranger. By 6.30pm my uncle had arrived with my grandparents. Full of surprise, my Uncle Mick was overwhelmed with hugs, kisses, and gifts from everyone. The drinks flowed, laughs roared, and bums were shaking on the dancefloor. Suddenly the music changed

to a Marilyn Monroe song. The spotlight focused on Mick as the DJ instructed him to take a seat on stage. Giggles, whispers, and curiosity could be heard around the room with searching eyes raised high, like a mob of meerkats. Out of nowhere, a slim, half-naked kissogram had appeared in front of him. Laughs and whistles cried out as Mick became giddy like a teenage boy. Flirting and brushing against him in white lingerie, I imagine that was the closest my uncle ever got to a woman's warm thighs, being the way he was. The night had gone down without a hitch.

Around 8pm, shortly after all the fun had started, the phone started ringing behind the bar.

"Is there a Peter here?" The barman shouted. Echo's of my dad's name went around the room.

"Peter, phone, quick," my grandma shouted.

Manoeuvring around people and tables, my dad made it to the phone!

"Hello is that Peter?"

"Yes, that's me."

"You're partner Angela has just given birth, and she wants you to come to the hospital."

"I'm coming now."

"Well?" My gran said, stood behind him.

"She's given birth."

7

My grandma turned around. "Quick... Mick, Kevin, get your jackets, we're going to the hospital, Angela has given birth."

"Birthday boy is driving."

"We will be back soon."

My dad and Mick headed to the car park with my grandparents. Being that Mick was t-total, he was the designated driver for the night while everyone got drunk. He didn't mind. After all, he was the only person over eighteen who wasn't drinking. The drive was short to the Workhouse Hospital for maternity. On arrival, one of the nurses pointed them to the correct room. Long hallways with faint cries came from both sides of the landing, by little bundles of joy. My mum was sat up holding a baby, as my dad and family quietly greeted and smiled, asking if she was ok.

"It's a boy" my mum revealed.

"Aww, brilliant." My family grasped with nice comments, smiles, and amazement gawking over her.

"Congratulations to both of you."

"What are you going to call him?"

"Joseph"

"Aww, baby Joseph."

"Well, we will leave you to get some rest."

My grandad eagerly ushered everyone back to the car. His Whiskey back at the club was getting lonely. Back to the club it was, to celebrate and share the good news with everyone. I

8

had just gatecrashed my Uncle Micks birthday. We now share the same day. It would have been great if I made it to the party, but for now, I was getting used to breathing the delightfully, fresh, antiseptic air from my cotton-wrapped swaddle.

I was going on four when I first started gathering memories. My third memory was me, sat in the kitchen sink as my mum bathed me. My brother Chris walked through the front door with his 80's multicoloured shell-suit and asked mum if she had some money. My first memory imprinted on my brain was when Chris ran halfway up the stairs, shaped like a sideways 'V,' just as I took my wet nappy off. He looked up at me and shouted; "mum, Joseph has taken his nappy off and ate his own shit." I was shocked, confused and agitated at such a lie. He wasn't even on the same landing as me. He could barely see my todger through the bannister as he looked up. The lie was scandalous. He told all his friends that I took my nappy off and ate my shit. It felt so wrong to say something that wasn't true. I must have been four, and that memory is as fresh as a daisy; what a Bastard. My second memory which I will never forget was when my mum got me out of the bath. Stood on my towel in front of the TV down in the living room, she rubbed baby oil all over me. Big-mouth-Chris was sat on the sofa right next to me. Mum thought it would be a good idea to pull my foreskin back so she could put baby lotion on. She had trouble pulling it back again.

Maybe it wasn't meant to be pulled back in the first place. When she finally tampered with my goods, the skin felt uncomfortably tight. There was a sudden panic from mum that interrupted the TV I was watching.

"Chris, I can't pull it back."

Hands slipping everywhere from the baby oil, panic had set in. I became more anxious and scared every second.

"Chris help me; I can't pull it back."

"I'm not touching that, what am I supposed to do."

My manhood was being strangled along with the fear my foreskin would be stuck permanently. By that point, I was screaming and crying as I looked down. Their lack of knowledge of what to do was not helping the situation. Tears rolled down my face. The TV had become a blurry, pixelated square. The fear took over me. What if it stuck like that forever? What if the doctor has to chop it off? How would I pee?

"Pleaseeee pull it back. Why did you do it in the first place?"

All sorts of crazy stuff went through my head. Out of all the people in that situation, I have a mum that doesn't know what she's doing, and a brother staring at the television with no sympathy. The worst part is knowing your family can't help. Finally, she managed to pull it back to normal. I felt like a trapped whitetail deer escaping from captivity. I just wanted to run and jump back into my natural surroundings under my bed

Those first years of life were already filled with highs and lows. I was a nervous wreck living with my mum and half-brother; not a very good half either. I used to fear my brother because he chased me around my room holding both corners of my duvet blanket high up before smothering me with it, frightening my short-lived life half to death. "Go in my room, and I will kill you!" That was his regular threat in case I ever forgot. I used to stay out of his way, the times that we did cross each other's path. I enjoyed watching him on our upstairs landing while he played with his big toy cars; Replicas of Ferrari and Aston Martin. He would lie on his side with his palm against his cheek, moving the cars around with his free hand. Although I stayed away from his room, the curiosity got the best of me. One day when he was out, his bedroom door was wide open. It was neat and tidy with his sports cars correctly parked in a straight line by his window. I heard someone enter the house, so I moved away quickly.

"Joseph, come here. I want to show you a magic trick."

I ran downstairs with excitement. My Brother was holding my favourite video 'Watch with Mother.' It was a black and white collection of children's programmes from the 1950s, through to the 1970s. He placed the video underneath the couch.

"I can magically disappear your video, and make it reappear under your bed cover."

"Go on then."

"The trick is complete; you may now go upstairs to look under your bed cover."

I ran upstairs as quick as I could to lift my blanket.

"Wow! How did you do that?" I asked with wonder.

"I told you, it's magic."

Convinced my brother was playing tricks on me, I asked him to do it again. He repeated the process to send the video back downstairs.

"Oh my God, you can do magic."

To this day, I never knew how he did it. My only guess is that he had two of the same videos without me knowing, and one of his sketchy friends hidden.

Life was good in Astley Village. We lived in a three-bedroom semi-detached house in a town called Chorley, ten miles from Preston. Our village was a council estate full of small doll-like sized houses that looked the same. To me, it was a big adventurous maze where I could free roam on foot. There was only one way in for cars. Running over small, grassy areas and darting down pathways and ginnels to get around, had become the norm. It was one big playground. Surrounded by streams, fields and tree's, you surprisingly couldn't get lost. All you had to do was walk in a straight line. Sooner or later you would end up on the main road, or in a

familiar part. Most of it looked the same. Even I kept getting confused whenever I took a wrong turn. We had the essentials nearby such as a primary school, a few shops and a local pub convenient for low-income families. The village was situated close to working-class homes. The main road lead to slip roads for cars that came in and out of Chorley. The only way to the rest of the world was through a large park behind the shops that lead straight into Chorley town centre. It was a scenic route whenever we couldn't afford the bus fare, but mainly because of the sizeable makeshift bird sanctuary halfway into the park. I loved watching the Peacocks flaunt their multi-coloured feathers in the shape of a rainbow, with what looked like eyes looking back at me. We also passed Astley Hall, the historical Tudor house. The hall was built sometime after 1576 by the Charnock family during the reign of Queen Elizabeth I. I imagine it was hard being Catholic at the time of a protestant queen. Looking up at the original leaded window, you can imagine how the people worshipped in private with a priest secretly conducting a mass. Now it's just a museum with everything still intact.

The village was great, built for summers for kids my age. Mum was a sociable drinker, and my brother never had any issues fitting in. As long as I can remember, I was never short of friends every time I went out. Everybody knew each other. You only had to come out of your front door before bumping into someone you knew. Only the best community came from

a tight-knit village. My dad was not around at the time. I don't know if Chris ever saw his dad. Life was easy, simple, and fun; the only time of normality I had with my mum. Chris was more fortunate than me; he was the only witness of any regularity shown by mum, way before I arrived. For some reason, I don't have many memories of her. I can't remember having any hugs or kisses as an average child would. I can't even remember what her young face looked like. There are memories around her, but for some reason, her face seems censored out like the maid in Tom & Jerry. Chris was in and out like a yo-yo. Being ten years older than me, he was coming up to Sixteen, and with no other men around the house, he was his own boss. All three of us never spent time together. We would go out, do our own thing with our personal friends, and then rendezvous back at the house whenever.

Just outside our house before it was time to go in, I was coasting around tight bends with great ease on my bike. The maze of pathways had plenty of dips and corners for my very useful stabilisers. Leaning into corners was second to none. Mum must be having a drink tonight. Her friend came outside to say hello to me during one of my many laps around the block.

"You will never learn how to ride unless you take your stabilisers off."

"But I can't ride without them."

14

"I'll take them off for you and show you how to do it."

I tried my best to convince her not to do it. There she was dismantling my bike with a pair of pliers. I was mortified. Coasting around was the best ever. My bike now in pieces, what was this drunk woman doing to it? I looked in sadness in what felt like forever. God knows what mum was doing inside.

"Right, come over here on this straight path. Now, you sit on the bike like you normally do, and I'm going to hold you upright."

"I want my mum to show me."

"She will come in a minute."

Looking over the woman's shoulder as she propped me up, mum was nowhere in sight.

"Now, you steer and peddle while I gently push you forward."

I knew this was only going to work if we did it together so I cycled as hard as I could. The bike was all over the place; I couldn't control it. Her left hand was on my handlebar, and her right hand was under my seat pushing. Three attempts later after being catapulted, I somehow managed to steer and balance to the end of the path raising my eyebrows, with the tip of my tongue out from excitement. I turned around and smiled at mums friend. She cheered and smiled back before vanishing behind the bush. I looked at the floor and pondered. Why did mum stay inside while her friend taught me how to ride a bike? I couldn't understand why. Why

didn't she show me instead of her friend? She didn't even watch.

Mum had a lot of friends in the village. Other single mums were in similar positions. Once you knew one family, being introduced to their friends was just a matter of time, and so it went on. Mums main friend was Irene. I was really good friends with her son and daughter, Ben and Tanya who were my age. I stayed at her house often. The mums had a babysitting rotor so that one of them could go out drinking for the night. I imagine my mum was either in the local pub or went to Preston. I had no idea what she got up to. She might as well have been a silent partner in a business. Only the business just happens to be my childhood. When it was time to come back inside, Irene wanted to relax in her living room, so we were all ordered to stay upstairs. We had some good laughs too. Ben and Tanya had sibling rivalry which was heightened with my presence. We all played together most of the time, but Tanya was my best friend. Ben would usually go off on his own escapades. Me and Tanya were like chalk and cheese, always stuck together. There was no good technology back then or any good toys, so we reverted to in-depth conversations. Three became a crowd, and they knew we would mess around all night, so we split up. Irene was a bit of a hothead. She went ballistic one day when all three of us ploughed through sixteen packets of crisp. There was never usually more than two of us in one room come

bedtime. Naturally, I always stuck with Tanya. Irene sure did have a mighty screech with her temper, as well as a really annoying voice that we didn't want to hear twice. Our bedroom light had to be switched off, but the landing light stayed on. I sat against the wall by the door, placing my head in the path of the light that entered through the gap. Any footsteps heard coming up the stairs, and we would quietly climb in bed pretending to be asleep. Once the coast was clear, we returned to our positions. Tanya had a nice view out of her back window. I could only see a few tree's and homes just over the back, but it looked good none-the-less.

"Oh my god, is that a UFO?" I pointed out.

"I don't think so," Tanya replied.

In the distance just over the backs, I could see lights around a shape. Imagination can run wild when you think and look hard enough. Tiredness had set in, so we climbed into the same bed for an expected sleep.

Time went much slower for me during the week. I went to Nursery a few times on and off, which was directly across from the local Primary School. Time couldn't pass fast enough. It was Summer during the six weeks holidays, so everyone was off school. Most of the time I would see a new drama in each part of the village as I roamed around alone. Chris would hang around with his group of friends sometimes outside the house. We had a small slope on the

front by the neighbour's house, where his gang of friends would sit in a row like blue tits perched together. I never got close to Chris or his inner circle for apparent reasons. The main reason being that I wasn't welcome. He had a close friend that stuck out from the rest called Dean. That particular day, Dean was about to fight with another lad near our home. I could overhear the conversation about how he never fought anyone and didn't want to partake. That was how arguments were settled I guess. Seeing Chris in his natural surroundings was like trying to track a nocturnal animal. He had a friend that lived a few doors away. Just by our house was a patch of grass in the middle of surrounding homes. Occasionally, Chris with two of his friends would march onto the green carrying a large white marquee tent. Rolled up like a carpet, they would sprawl it out. It covered all of the grass and was filled with graffiti. Shuffling around on their knees with felt pens, they carried on what they had started. It was pretty cool to watch. I tried my luck asking if I could write my name on it, getting a quick response that was opposite to yes!

I loved climbing trees. Going off for hours looking for anything to climb, even if it wasn't a tree, was all I wanted to do. Being small and agile, climbing and exploring was my thing. Just across from my front door, I could see two small trees. A branch stuck out, begging me to hang upside down like a bat. Looking towards the ground, I imagined what

would happen if the branch snapped. Moments later I heard a snap! Hurtling towards the earth, I landed smack-bang on the top of my head, nearly breaking my neck. Everything went blurry. Crying my eyes out, I laid on the floor helpless. From around the corner, a woman appeared and placed me in her arms to carry me home. I felt as sick as a dog. Mum answered the door, and the exchange was made. One of the many accidents I had as a kid. I was never out of the hospital. The doctor commented on how he had never seen so many head x-rays for a kid. My knees had also taken damage over the summer, from trying to cycle down steep hills at fifteen miles per hour with my tiny wheels. That was around the time I woke up in my mum's bed paralysed. Having nothing to do with all my accidents, I woke up one day unable to feel my legs. Not knowing what was wrong, I crawled out of bed with my arms towards the landing. Mum was fast asleep, so I left her be. At the top of the landing, my arms were exhausted. Getting downstairs would be impossible.

"Mum, help me!"

"What are you doing on the floor."

"I can't feel my legs, help me."

Knowing straight away something was seriously wrong, she carried me into the car to take me to the hospital. My grandparents met us both in the Chorley hospital car park worried sick. It turned out I dislocated my hip. For the next week, I laid in a hospital bed with my legs sticking up in the air. bandages attached to weights kept pulling me down the

bed. The nurses told me to stay on my back during the night. Come morning, two nurses spent an hour every day unravelling me from the twisting and turning I did. My grandad sat in an armchair nearly every night watching over me. A girl across from me had the same problem, becoming my friend for the week. After recovering, I was back to my usual self with my clicky hip.

My life expectancy over the holidays was at a whole time low. Even my cat became a victim when he was run over. It was Tanya that came to tell me. Around the back of our house, the road was on a bend. Cars went fast without giving any thought; Poor thing. My life nearly ended when my mum bought me a pair of red wellington boots. Ideally, they were meant to be for winter. I loved them so much that I walked around with them all summer. My mum laughed at me and told everyone. The stream was very close to our house, so I went to see how waterproof they were. Two girls older than me were climbing on a rope swing over the water, so I moved further down. Life was great. The sun was shining down on me as I splashed in the shallow water. There was a hedge beside me that towered high. Two or three flies buzzed by. Maybe the water was dirty. I didn't imagine so; the water was spotless. Splashing was great, but the swing looked better. They looked like they were having fun. Confidence was not my strong point. I was scared of my own shadow. After a few minutes, the flies became more frequent. I looked up

towards the top of the hedge to see a whole swarm of bees, flying straight at me. Sharp pains covered my body as I tried to fend them off. Each sting was like a sharp pinprick. Only wearing shorts, t-shirts and my wellington boots, I was utterly overwhelmed. Stood screaming on the spot, I could just about make out two figures in front of me. The two girls dragged me out of the water. Carrying me in her arms, one of them took the lead to get me home. I must have told them where I lived in hysterics. Once again, my mum was meeting me at the front door with my new war wounds. Sat on the kitchen counter with only my shorts, my mum rubbed a pink lotion over every sting. My entire body was full of red spots. I looked like I had Chickenpox for a second time, which would have been rare. It was safe to say that I wasn't allergic to bee stings!

I learnt about the birds and bees when I stayed at one of my friend's house. Erika was a girl that lived across from Ben and Tanya. Summer was over, and I was starting my first day at primary school the next day. Erika was a year older than me, and a year above me in my new school. Mum thought it would be a good idea if she took me to school for my first day. It would have been better if I knew someone in the same class as me. Our mums were downstairs drinking and laughing that night. We had to stay upstairs so we could start winding down for a planned early night. We had fun trying on each other's school uniform, then going downstairs to

show our mothers, who found it just as funny. I had no ambition to be a girl; it was just amusing. There was only one television downstairs, so we had to make our own entertainment. We kept sneaking down earwigging the conversation, and having a peek to see what's on TV. It must have been a late-night movie because there was some kind of sex scene. They heard us giggling, then shouted us back upstairs. Erika said they were having sex, but I was none the wise. That was the first sight and knowledge about sex I had seen, which was just a man and woman kissing in bed.

"Let's have sex," Erika suggested.

"How?"

"First we take off all our clothes, and then you lie on top of me."

I don't know what she knew, but I had no idea what sex was. Getting in bed, I did as she told me.

"You have to move up and down like this."

I didn't see the fascination rubbing up and down, naked on top of a girl.

"I'm getting tired; I'm having a rest."

"Don't go to sleep; I want to do it again."

"I don't want to anymore."

She was getting angry, so I had to do it again. All it did was tire me out, hurt my arms and made me hot.

"I'm going to sleep now," I told her.

She wasn't happy at all. Soon after I was fast asleep. The next morning on the way to school, she didn't talk to me. She was in a mood because I didn't carry on, but to me, it was pretty pointless. The whole way there, she walked a few feet in front, ignoring me. So much for my first day at school. I don't know where my mum was.

My first week at primary school went with a bang. I didn't know where I was supposed to go, Erika wouldn't even point me in the right direction after shouting her name. I had to ask another kid, then finally a teacher took me to my new class. It was the first room just by the main entrance; nice and easy to find. I was nervous and shy keeping quiet all the time. All the kids sat on cushioned bean bags in front of the teacher. The tall female instructed us to get into pairs before starting an activity over by the knee-high desk. I didn't know anyone or felt like joining in so I decided to stay where I was to feel sorry for myself, hoping the lovely lady would show a profound understanding on my first day. The teacher asked me to join in, but I just refused, staring at the floor with my bottom lip hanging down. The day after I was feeling the same, and acted the same. The teacher left the room momentarily. Ten minutes later, the headmaster walked in and looked at me. Only then had I clicked on that she had summoned him for me.

"Stand up! Come with me."

Following his instructions, we both walked down the corridor, me in front of him, frog-marching towards his office. At the end of the hallway were two red doors that swung both ways. Suddenly losing my breath, I was airborne flying through the air before sliding along the tiled floor on my belly, right towards a red coat of paint. The doors opened as I crashed into them head first. Before I knew what was going on, he picked me up by the scruff of my neck and dragged me to his office like a rag doll. In complete shock, I just kept walking. Another lad was standing in the corner facing the wall. I wonder if he felt the same wrath as me. He told me to stand against a pillar that supported the roof of his office. I could see from the corner of my eye there were two headmasters. They were working side by side on a desk. I was even more scared knowing there were two of them. After standing against that wall all day, my stomach was killing me. Not moving a muscle, the bell finally vibrated, signalling my freedom from a crazy headmaster, that acted as if nothing had happened. My new teacher must really hate me. I was so relieved to get home. That was the first and last day I remember of that school. That day taught me that life was no fun and games.

Most weekends my grandad picked me up and drove me to Preston to stay with my gran and Uncle Mick. My grandad worked in Chorley, so it was easy for him to pick me up. I loved staying at their house. I slept in Mick's bed at night

time. He was like a dad, an uncle and a best friend rolled into one. There was a room for my gran's sewing machine next to his bedroom. I was hoping for it to be turned into my bedroom one day. My dad was still absent. I had no memories of him whatsoever. He smashed all the windows on mums car for some reason. Driving around with no windows was draughty. Eventually, the car had to go. Maybe there was more than meets the eye as to why dad lives away. I certainly needed a dad to protect me from bees and Headmasters'. Christmas soon came around. Mum couldn't afford a tree when we first moved in, so me and Tanya drew a tree on the living room wall that wasn't decorated. This year we manage to get one. The only time I can remember spending time with mum, was when we put the tree up that year. We did the lights and decorations together, but I kept going into the kitchen to get more crackers to eat, adding extra butter to the point of feeling sick.

For whatever reason, we had to move house by the time I was six. I think mum wanted to be closer to Preston. I don't know if my dad played a part. It was unfortunate to leave Chorley. For me, it was the worst mistake mum could ever make. I loved where we lived. We went to view a house on a farm in Leyland, situated between Chorley and Preston. The house was on the main road, next to the farmer's main house. Besides the smell of cow manure, it was pretty old and run down. I don't know what the hell she was thinking.

Around the back was a large barn full of hay and cattle, and acres of land with planted vegetables. Maybe she thought it would be cool to work on a farm. I had a feeling that we were taking the rented house regardless.

Chapter 2 - The Farmer's Son

Leaving Chorley pushed me, my brother and mum much closer to Preston. Mum had decided to take the rented farmhouse which was a major blow. I didn't know what to expect or how she found it but what a shithole. It was situated a mile from the town centre of Leyland, and not far from Preston. She should have kept going for another mile or two in either direction, that would have been perfectly fine by me. Her dad would have liked the idea of working on a farm, so there was some logic for the decision I guess. If she wanted to escape my dad, then she was going in the wrong direction. If it was all that we could afford, then that explained it. The farmer owned both properties but decided to rent out the one on the left; maybe for extra income. As soon as we arrived, the first thing we would notice was the smell. It stunk of cow shit. Not the best of moves by mum, but we didn't have a choice. The Farmer, Jim Wilding, lived in the house on the right with his wife and fifteen-year-old son, Steven Wilding; a name I would never forget. Jim's wife moved out a few weeks after we moved in. It had to be aweful if the farmer's wife was leaving. Farm life with that smell could strip any woman's dignity. You could buy all the perfume on the shop shelf, and you still wouldn't mask that shit! She was probably waiting for someone to rent the house before leaving; releasing her into her environment of a woman's life, not a farmer's life.

We soon settled in and quickly got into a routine. Mum got me into the local primary school half a mile down the lane. She had a bicycle with a child seat on the back so she could take me to school in the freezing mornings. Mum had a new friend around the corner, whose son went to the same school as me. I don't know how she met friends other than sharing an interest like drinking; unless she met them on my school playground. I started to get free lifts in the morning because they owned a car. Mum couldn't be bothered taking me anymore. Once again, I was palmed off on somebody else. I never really settled in or made any good friends from that school, especially being the new kid. It's hard being the new face when everyone already knows each other.

The positive about living on the farm was that my dad started to come around. Maybe my mum and dad were friends again. He would have been a familiar face to me from birth, so having him around every so often went unnoticed as a young child, but as I got older memories of him began to phase in. Where he came from, I didn't know. I just instinctively knew that this man was my dad. Chris, on the other hand, was seen less and less. Having different dads might have complicated things, but being sixteen, he was probably out doing his own thing. My dad came to visit me at school during one of my dinner breaks, that surely surprised me, along with a confidence boost. Stood on the yard, I heard

someone shout something, then thought nothing of it. Unaware with decibels well over one hundred from all the screaming kids, some girl on the yard told me that a man was shouting my name. As I turned around, my dad was waving at me in his black leather jacket. Being 6 feet, 4 inches tall, you couldn't miss him. He came to visit us from Preston from time to time, just nothing permanent. To me, life started in Chorley, and now we are making our way back to Preston as a whole. There must be more to it; I was just too young to understand. It was good to see dad during that time, mainly because I didn't know anyone in school. I loved my dad. He was a good-looking, relaxed guy from what I saw. I just never saw him as much as I would have liked. That day when I got home, I asked him for 50p to get some chocolate. There were no shops nearby apart from a petrol station across the main road, so I asked dad if I could go. He wouldn't let me because it was too dangerous. He also wasn't in the mood to take me after begging him. The legal tender in my pocket might as well be worthless if I can't get a delicious chocolate bar. I hung around the farm with my shiny silver coin, deciding what I should buy if I managed to get to a shop. Dads voice was repeating in my head; "Don't you dare go to that garage on your own." I was stuck between a rock and a hard place. I sauntered around for a few minutes around the back of the house, opposite the barn thinking dad would stay inside. The garage was so close I could taste it, along with cow manure in the back of my throat. If I ran quick, I could be home before he noticed I was gone; then I

will hide the chocolate in my pocket. My need for something sugary was far greater than any consequence. When I got there, I bought a mint aero which cost precisely 50p; a good deal on my part. On the way back, and back on the right side of the road, I was making good time, so I ate one piece. Barely finishing that one piece, I looked up to see my dad marching straight towards me with a sour face. "I told you not to go!" He shouted, before taking my chocolate off me.

That night, dad seemed to be staying. Mum ran a bath for me before bedtime. Shortly after getting into the tub, dad came upstairs to brush his teeth. I'm glad someone showed up because mum wasn't good at making appearances. I stood up and asked if I could brush my teeth at the same time, but was told to sit down or I would slip.

"Brush them after; you will break your neck."

When he went downstairs, I disobeyed him for the second time that day. I stood up and leaned over to brush my teeth by the sink, just like dad did. Like most bathrooms in Britain, the bath, the sink, and toilet are packed together. Stood on the edge of the tub in all my glory leaning over, I brushed away. Ten seconds later I slipped forward and smashed my skull against the porcelain sink. My right eyebrow split clean open before ending up on my ass next to the toilet. I screamed in agony. Dad sprinted upstairs to scoop me up.

"Jesus Christ, what have you done?"

Being so tall, he was at the top of the stairs in three steps. I sat downstairs in a white towel in mum's arms while we waited for an ambulance looking like Rocky Balboa. The sickness feeling reminded me from the time I landed on the top of my head. Being six, I was amazed not to have killed myself. Making it to seven would be an achievement on its own.

After recovering from my bad fall, I soon realized there was not much to do in my spare time. We lived on the main road with a few streets that lead off into dead ends, so it wasn't exactly like I could go anywhere; one way in and one way out. I met one or two new friends that lived around the corner, but they never really classed me as a friend. I was an outsider; someone they didn't know. It was the result of moving house. If they played in each other's home, I was excluded. I didn't mind because I was a content type of kid, unaware of any bad in the world. Bad vibes came from them the time they locked up their bike against a lamp post. The lock had a four-digit password that was only to be known by them. The feeling left me rather sad. My rented friends and I played out one summer's day when we decided to play near a stream. The stream was at the bottom of a very steep bank, covered with nettles; a death trap if anyone was to fall, even if it was only a few feet down. We all stood on the edge, simulating the consequences if one of us were to fall in. Everyone had moved away from the edge, but I stayed

looking down. Now, I wasn't sure if they pushed me or if I fell, but before I knew it, I was tumbling head over heels through the nettles, hurtling straight towards the stream. The pain was terrible. Face planted at the bottom of the dirty water, I flicked my head back opening my eyes. The murky water splashed past my head in slow motion as I tried to pick myself up. Bushes and a fence were on my right side. The only way out was back up through the nettles. Screaming in pain, the two boys looked freaked out. It was Chorley all over again. How can a stream become so dangerous? Stood in shorts and t-shirts, I looked up to see the boys waving a large stick to pull me back up. I climbed up enough to reach the stick with my hands. Climbing back through the nettles was absolute hell. Tears poured down my face. Climbing blind, I slipped and ended up straight back into the water. On the second attempt, I finally came to the top with my survival instinct to survive beyond six. Going through the nettles four times left my body covered in stings. The boy's status changed to friends for saving me. Maybe they weren't so bad after all presuming they didn't push me in. It happened that fast, it wasn't worth going over. My house was a few hundred yards away, but luckily my bike was with me. I jumped on to pedal home fast. Soaking wet and in complete agony, tears continued to make my vision blurry. Talk about déjà vu. I had to take a bath before mum could apply her magic pink lotion again. The bath was black from being so dirty. The pain for the following hour was like a thousand knives stabbing me all over. Being in the wars seemed like a regular

occurrence for me. Most kids are lucky to fall over and graze their knee. Every time I go out seems to be a car crash waiting to happen.

Chris came back when my dad was gone, and mum was warming up pea and ham soup for tea. She made it the day before, but I kept my complaints to myself. At six, it didn't take much food to fill me up anyway. The kitchen was in the living room where mum prepared the food. We had an old-fashioned fireplace that burned wood inside. Very therapeutic to watch once it got going. Starting it with paper and wood was a real pain. Walking from behind the counter, mum gave Chris the bowl of soup.

"Soup again? I had this yesterday. I don't want soup; I want a fucking meal."

Mum was trying to explain how we didn't have much in. Chris stood up and threw the bowl of soup at the wall opposite my couch before storming out of the house. The green wallpaper now had a new tint of green. I just sat still while it rained pea & ham soup. Once Chris left, mum just sighed and carried on wiping the surface with a flat look on her face, after briefly pausing.

I didn't know much about my mum; what she did during the day or what kind of person she was. She sometimes left me with the farmer's wife next door while she went out for a few

hours. His wife was a lovely woman; you could tell she was a proper mother by the way she carried herself. I went shopping with her that day, and we talked about general stuff. I felt like I could talk to her about anything. The strange thing was, I had more conversation and connection with the farmer's wife in one hour than I could ever remember having with mum. She let me pick what food I wanted for my tea from the supermarket freezer. When mum came to get me, I didn't want to leave. I started to wish that she was my mum instead. The day she moved off the farm was sad. We all said goodbye to her on the front of the house; her car was parked on the main road ready to go. I gave her a big hug like usual being very fond of her, making it clear how I felt.

We got to know the farmer and his family well. Mum even got stuck in and milked the cows, doing odd jobs to knock some rent off. She started leaving me next door more often while she went out for a few hours. The Farmer and his son were busy all day around the back, so I was in and out messing around. She must have thought I'd be fine if the Wildings kept an eye on me. I would usually walk over to the cow's pen to feed them grass or hay, playing tug of war with their long tongues. One of the bulls escaped one day chasing Chris to the big steel gate. I'd never seen him move so fast in my life. Stood by the back door, I laughed my ass off. One of the cows ended up dying soon after moving in. It was no

wonder with Chris around provoking them, but sad none the less. Jimmy and Steven dug a big hole right near our back door, then they dragged its corpse with the tractor to the hole. It was uncomfortable knowing a dead cow was buried so close to the back door. Apart from my cat getting run over, that was the second time I experienced death. After a month or so living there, we got used to the smell of cow manure. My clothes, on the other hand, would linger in class. Not only was I a loner, but I stunk of cow shit. The kids thought I was pretty cool once they knew I lived on a farm. Other kids lived on farms as well, stinking right along with me. It still didn't stop some kids making fun. If I weren't hanging around watching smelly cattle or avoiding where I stood ever since I stood on a rusty nail in the backyard, then I would go inside waiting for something to happen. One day something did happen. Events that would change my life forever.

Steven was only fifteen by the time he was driving their big green tractor to fields they farmed not far away. He was so cool and lucky to drive a massive tractor with tyres as tall as my dad. One day he asked me if I wanted to go for a ride. Without hesitation, I jumped straight in. He sat me on his leg while we drove on the main road, being that there was only one seat. My friends in Chorley wouldn't believe me if I told them. What a privilege. It was fascinating too, being so high up, looking down on all the traffic. I reckon Chris was jealous. We drove to some fields nearby where he briefly

stopped to open a few gates so that the cows could change fields. After that, we soon headed back. My mum seemed fine leaving me more regularly with Steven. Numerous tractor rides later, he asked me if I wanted to go with him again. I loved going on the main road so why not. We drove down a muddy trail surrounded by trees, close to where he took me the first time. He pulled up on a steep bank in a densely, rural place with trees all around. "Wait here because I want to show you something," he ordered. As I stood there, he started climbing the steep bank, pulling himself up by the thin trees. After twenty minutes I began to wonder what he was doing. Twenty minutes lasted forever in such a scary overgrown wooded area. Soon after, he came over the top with a calf in his arms and carefully climbed down towards me. Why has he brought a calf, I thought? Steven stood behind the calf, without saying a word to me. Without even looking at me, he started to pull his pants down as I stood confused. He grabbed its short tail, lifted it up and put his penis inside one of its orifices. I didn't know what to think. Was this normal? My brain went into overdrive to try and figure out why he was doing such a thing. Not knowing much about the world, all I could do was watch. I knew something was wrong. It couldn't be clean, doing that to a cow. I knew what Erika showed me in Chorley last year was normal because we watched it on TV, but this didn't seem right. There just weren't any answers I could come up with. After he had finished having sex, he told me to wait while he took the poor calf back up the steep bank to release it. I had to

remain there, worried about what was going to happen when he got back. When he did get back, thankfully we climbed back into the tractor to head home. The conversation was dead the whole way back. He was talking to me, but I couldn't hear a word as I sat silently and uncomfortably on his knee. "Promise that you won't tell anyone what you saw," he repeated. After what he showed me, how could I possibly explain to anyone? I'd get in big trouble if I told mum, so I kept it to myself. It was a naughty thing to do. Equivalent to witnessing a murder in the mind of a six-year-old.

I stayed indoors after what happened to avoid our backyard where Steven and his dad tended to. My absence was short lived when Steven caught me. He asked me to go with him again. I told him I didn't want to go. "I want to show you a cool den that I've built." I was hoping he might not repeat what he did last time, praying it was a one-off, so I went along; dens were my favourite. He took me back in the tractor to an open field that his dad owned. After a short walk, we came across a small, stone hut; you could tell it was handmade. It looked like a small bomb shelter, made out of rocks piled upon one another with some partial laid brick. He left a gap for a doorway and a window as a lookout. "What are you going to use it for," I innocently asked. He told me he was going to bring cows here, and it was also a place we could go in the future once he's finished building it. I was starting to realize his agenda. He wasn't interested in

anything else which got me worried. What plans did he have for me? Was he going to do to me, what he does to cows? I asked myself. As life went on, I did my best to stay away from the strange lad. Chris would never do the sort of things Steven did.

Mum had to go out one day that caused me to stay next door in the farmer's house. Steven naturally took advantage by offering to be the one that watched me. I wanted to tell her what kind of stuff he was doing, but I was more worried about getting in trouble. When I got to his house, he took me to his bedroom where his dog was asleep on his white bed sheets. We sat down and started talking in his dull house with hardly any possessions, and no characteristics whatsoever. He would tell me how he used to have sex with his dog when he was younger, but now he couldn't because his penis wouldn't fit. As he told me this, he picked up his dog, pulled his pants down and motioned in front of me to give an example of how he did it. Still unaware of how bad the situation was, I still had no answers for myself. Maybe this is what older boys did? I asked him what other animals he had tried it with to avert his attention on me. His cat was asleep on the bed, so I asked if he's tried it with a cat. "It's too small." He said. I couldn't think of anything else to say, so I stayed on the end of the bed quietly turned towards the door ready to run. Those few hours lasted a lifetime. Before long I was able to go home when mum got back; another

close encounter. Pressure mounted in my mind. It was as if I could hear a train coming, but I couldn't see it.

Dad had gone AWOL again. Chris was probably staying with friends in Chorley. It was apparent that mum had little or no interest in me. Each chance she got, I was palmed off on someone else. After three uncomfortable situations with Steven, I continued to avoid him, but it seemed impossible when we lived on the same stinking farm. He had lived there all of his unnatural life. I just wished for it to be a pit stop. I reckon she found it in the paper when she was drunk. She always did think she was high and mighty after a few drinks, full of rhetoric. Maybe she felt like a challenge in a drunken state. The house sat empty for a good reason. If a house is empty, you have to ask why? My memories of her became scarce. I don't know what life she had. She could be like James Bond for all I knew working for the British government. She certainly had a cold calculated personality.

Steven wanted me to sleep at his cousins, but I firmly refused after knowing what he does to animals. I think he convinced my mum because for some reason I had to go. He tricked me by telling me we were going to get something of his. On the way, we passed the ditch I fell in. Night time would be a scary time to fall in, now the sun has gone. Once we got there, he revealed that we were sleeping. After a long walk through fields, I had no idea how to get back. Lying on the sofa, his

cousin watched television while I tried to reason with Steven to take me home. He knew there was nothing I could do. I couldn't even call for help if I needed to. The house was acres away from the nearest road. Eventually, his cousin went upstairs to his room, giving me some reassurance that he probably wasn't in on it. Soon after, we went to a small spare room at the back of the house. It soon became apparent the reason why he wanted me to sleep over. There in front of us was a single bed. I tried to get out of it and asked to sleep on the sofa, but he just told me his cousin stays up all night, even though he just went to bed. The fact that there were no adults in the house scared me. Telling him I want to go home failed because he stood by the bedroom door until he convinced me. Being in that house wasn't safe. There was no way to get back, and I knew what he wanted to do to me. To him, it was prom night. As we both got in bed, I started to panic. I insisted on sleeping on the end, close to the door where I could escape. I faced away from him because I didn't want to have his face in front of mine, or his stinking breath, breathing over my face. He did his best to make sure I got undressed. I made sure I kept my red underpants on. When I tried to go to sleep, I could feel his hand sliding my underpants down as he started to rub his penis against me. Every time he tried, I kept pulling them back up telling him to stop. I began to get angry as he repeated the process every time I nodded off. It was a losing battle, but no way is he doing to me, what he does to animals; Yuck!

"Come on; Just let me do it." The twisted teenager remarked.

The fight to try and stop him paid off after an hour. Eventually, he gave up and went to sleep. I was fortunate this time but how long could I prevent it? He's going to get me one day. Why does my family never seem to be around?

After a while, Steven started to leave me alone for some reason. I was glad but couldn't help feeling it was the calm before the storm. What plan did he have for me next? Long behold, he was back again hounding me. I wish he would leave me alone and stop harassing me. I was hanging around by the back door, getting some fresh air because the farm seemed quiet and Steven wasn't around. Out of the blue, the dirty lad appeared with his fixed emotionless face. He would look as if he was focusing on something behind me but knew exactly what he wanted. This time he tried to show me his new den that he made in the barn opposite the back of my house. At the end of the barn were stacks of hay piled up ready for winter. I didn't want to go, but he bribed me with sweets that waited for me once we got inside. "Come on it's cool; just come for a minute." Intrigued to see a den made of hay, filled with sweets, and close to home, I thought I would be safe. I doubt he would try anything, so I decided to walk over. We walked past the cows' pen and climbed up a stair created from a bale of hay. The den was in the corner high up. As he pulled a block of hay away, it revealed a secret entrance for us to climb in. We sat in there for a while having a general conversation, eating the sweets. The conversation

He rubbed himself against me, prodding me with his penis. Chris used to smother me with my blanket. This was a million times worse. The hay was getting on my chest. After doing what he said, I pulled my pants up trying to get out for some air. Luckily he didn't refuse, so we climbed out. Another close call! "Don't tell anyone," he repeated over and over again. I felt dirty and disgusting standing so close to him. Once home, I was just glad he didn't rape me. He had me trapped loads of times. I wanted to tell mum what he was doing, but Steven said if I did, he would blame it all on me and tell everyone it was all my idea. I didn't dare to tell anyone.

Life carried on as usual with mum and the farm like nothing was happening. No one had any idea what Steven was doing to me. He knew how to get me where he wanted, so I wasn't left with many options. It had become a battle of forces between his need, and my will not to. Something had to give sooner or later.

It became quiet with only me and mum around the house. She never let me sleep in her bed unless I had a nightmare. Staying long term in that house was not foreseeable. It was the plain, featureless house it's always been. Not one roll of wallpaper had gone up since we moved in. Occasionally, we had rats under the floorboards that Jimmy had to remove by ripping the entire living room floor up. The rats were as big

as cats, from such a healthy diet. Night time was hard to get any sleep. The only toys I had were a few small figures under my bed. We had to go to the dentist in the morning, so I had to go to sleep. Still no car, we walked through a wooded area back to civilisation in Leyland. The dentist was close to my school. I'd been for check-ups in the past, but this appointment was far from a check-up. I never liked the sharp bit they pressed against my gums; it made me freak out every time. We came to a compromise of only using the small mirror. The dentist man told me he had to give me a filling. Not thinking anything of it, he gently pressed a gas mask over my face to sedate me. Those were the years before Novocaine injections were introduced. Pushing the mask away, I felt like I couldn't breathe. It felt like being back in that barn between the bales of hay with Steven. Each time I pushed it away, the dentist man put the mask over my mouth.

"Can we get some more nurses in here please."

"Come on Joseph; you need to do it," mum said while rubbing my arm.

The bastard smothered me with the mask while four nurses held me down. I kicked, fought, and struggled until I passed out; not completely unconscious, just very drowsy. The pain as he drilled into my bottom right tooth was worse than falling through nettles and being attacked by bees put together. I could feel him push something hard into my tooth to fill it. I was traumatised. Mum didn't say anything on the

way home, or on the way there for that matter. My feeling towards her started to become negative. I could only ever weigh mum up whenever the farmer's wife came to visit. I hugged her every time. She was such a nice lady. It wasn't the same for my mum. If only they both knew what Steven was doing.

Hanging around the front of our house one day, the side gate was being opened so the tractor could come out. It was the dirty lad. Sometime later, Steven managed to find and manipulate me to go with him like he usually did. Other times I had to go while mum went out. This time we had to take the tractor to let the cows out. He didn't just let the cows out, he had sex with them first. I was sure this was the time he would hurt me. If I didn't tell anyone, how could I stop it? When we got there, he told me to wait while he climbed up the embankment to find another calf. As he disappeared over the tree line, I started to worry about what I was in for. The last occasion took him twenty minutes to catch one, so I had to think fast. He nearly raped me in the barn. After a moment, answers and solutions flooded my instinct. If I run home now, I could get there before he returned to his tractor. The plan seemed right, but something kept me back. Thinking too hard crashed my memory. He's going to come over that tree line any second if I don't run now. Something in the back of my tiny skull shouted RUN! As fast as I could, I sprinted down the long muddy trail surround by leaning

trees. They leaned straight towards me as if to stop me. Looking over my shoulder every two seconds, the main road was nearly before me. My small legs could barely keep up with my speed causing me to nearly trip over. Once on the main road, I eased off the gas catching my breath. I knew it was just a little bit further. My little heart was beating fast, but I had to keep going. I ran over a mile before I heard a large vehicle amongst all the passing traffic. I looked back to see a big monstrous tractor coming for me. Still in a quick march, I could hear it getting closer. As it reached the side of me, its huge wheels rolled straight past me. Thank god for that, it was someone else. There was no sign of Steven. When I got home, I frantically ran through the front door. My mum was in the kitchen cooking something, and I knew I had to tell her quickly. What if she hits me, I thought? I stood halfway up the stairs catching my breath, ready to run in the bathroom, the only room with a lock on the door. I shouted her numerous times through the wooden railing for her attention, getting her angry which was a sign that she was listening clearly.

"Mum, Steven put his willy into a cow's bum, and he tried to do it to me."

"WHAT!" She screamed.

I quickly ran into the bathroom and locked it shut. Mum had to convince me to come out after I made her promise not to smack me. Relief flooded my veins. She phoned the police where I was taken to the police station to be gently

questioned. Once Chris found out he chased Steven down the road to try and kick the shit out of him, but he ran like a coward. My dad, on the other hand, chased Jimmy down the road, dragged him out of his tractor and beat him up. I later found out they had a fire that completely burnt the barn down by someone who will remain anonymous. It was good to hear they lost something out of this ordeal, even if it was only a few thousand pounds. It still didn't replace my innocence or dignity. After what he did, I was just glad he never got the chance to rape me. If I didn't run that day, who knows what he had planned. Steven Wilding still lives on his farm with his dad on Leyland Lane, Leyland, Preston. They still rent out their spare house next door. He denied everything of course during his interview, so there wasn't enough evidence to charge him. I was just glad to get out of that rat-infested shithole. Things were never the same after that. Steven still lives in the house on the right leading a happy life.

My strange, absent mum had let me down. I just didn't realise at the time.

Chapter 3 - Dad's Second Chance

With the farm gladly behind us, we all moved back to Preston. Back to where it all started. The only difference is, I was a newborn baby the last time I lived there. Dad managed to get a flat of his own, so mum and I moved in with him. It was good being together as a happy family. Chris was living somewhere else. I got the impression he never got on with my dad; they were never seen together. That could explain why we moved to Chorley in the first place. Now going on seven, it was time for a fresh start. Changing schools was the only downside. Every time I made new friends in a new school or town, we were on the move again. Life was boring alone. It was the first time I could spend some quality time with dad, other than just a quick hello. The flat was certainly cool. We lived on the second floor, of a three-story building shared with two other flats, close to the town centre. Situated on a corner, the living room windows enabled us to see the street and the main road. Just across the road were two pubs, and two shops all bunched up together. Along our corridor inside the flat were the kitchen, a bathroom, and one bedroom right at the end. It was different from having my own room. They had the king-size bed, while I was on a camp bed in the corner. Night time had to be the worst times ever. The flat never had any central heating, and the window was single glazed. Lying under the window with a thin sleeping bag, I was absolutely freezing! Just below us lived a really nice lady named Josie, who became a close family

friend. In the mornings, we would rise to the beautiful smell of sausages, bacon, and eggs being cooked in the café next door directly below us. It was indeed an improvement to smelling cow shit every day. Dad sometimes bought something in the mornings. When he did, he ordered a sausage butty; two sausages cut in half on white bread with oozing brown sauce all over. That was the damn finest thing I had ever eaten. I would sit on the floor in front of him watching his every last bite, as he sat on the sofa resting his ankle over his right knee in his usual posture. He only bought himself one. They both stayed at home all day, so I don't think we had much money. If I were lucky, he would let me have a bite, or even give me half. I would savour every last mouthful. Mum was always in and out of the living room, or in and out of the flat. She could never sit still and was a mystery to me. She seemed on the edge like she didn't feel comfortable in her own skin. I couldn't work her out.

Just like every move, there was a waiting period to get me into a new school; something I always loathed. It was a good spot where we lived, convenient for everything we needed; town, a large park, shops, churches, and public transportation were all within throwing distance. Unable to hang around the front of the house, or allowed to go out, all I could do was hang around mum and dad, and how exciting could that be. Dad took me for a walk into town to visit a church. Saint Wilfred's church was the most beautiful place I

had ever seen. Walking inside for the first time was unreal. Marble pillars stood tall on each side between gold chandeliers. Rows and rows of benches were laid straight to the front of the altar, where statues and ornaments surrounded the enormous crucifix of Jesus Christ. Walking in the foyer, dad showed me how to put holy water on my forehead, before lighting a candle. The clean smell of burning wax made me feel lethargically cleansed. The silence within the church could calm any storm within a man's heart. He seemed to like those candles. For some silly reason when he turned his back, I put two of them into my pocket. On the way home, I showed dad what I took for him. Unaware of the principle as to why we lit candles in the first place, he went mad and scolded me. I was in deep trouble. He took my hand and pulled me into a building of offices we stood next to. "I'm taking you to the police station." Scared out of my mind, I begged him not to. "Can I speak to a police officer; my son has been stealing." He said to the lady over the counter. She looked at me, then said "ok" to my dad before walking off. Looking at dad, he looked suspiciously comfortable leaning against the desk on his side, with one leg behind the other. He made me promise him never to steal again; I agreed. "Come on let's go." He must have winked at her to play along. It was a smart lesson to teach me. I had no plans to steal after that day.

It was good being around both parents. It gave me a sense of security. Days passed, and nights came without doing much throughout the day. Mum and I might nip to town, while dad used to go out. Being close to plenty of pubs, we sometimes went for a drink during the day. I would have half a pint of coke or lemonade, while they had a pint of beer. By dinner time it was really quiet. Older locals would read their paper, smoking a cigarette with one hand, turning the pages with the other, as they licked their yellow, nicotine coloured fingers. On one occasion from boredom, I began biting on my glass. Mum and dad started bickering about god-knows-what. I bit so hard that a piece of glass broke off in my mouth. In front of me was an empty glass with a perfect bite mark the shape of my rounded teeth; pretty impressive for a seven-year-old. Dad freaked out with his hand in front of my mouth like he was feeding a horse. "Spit it out, quick." That was the highlight of our life I guess, going to the pub for a mouth full of glass. What else was there to do for people. Unemployment was high, families lived on the breadline, and technology hadn't got going. Dad was a fully qualified mechanic, while mum had been an auxiliary nurse. It wasn't that they couldn't work; they just chose not to. They chose to drink instead. We got to know a few people living on the edge of an estate. Now I know mums secret to making friends. It was pretty cool seeing such animated people drunk by 1pm. The same faces would come and go. There was one man that used to make me laugh. 'Stan the man' was a big old guy on the doorstep of the pub smoking. He always wore a long grey

checkered overcoat with his white mop hairstyle, and numerous teeth missing. Laughing and joking all the time, you would hear him before seeing him. No one would imagine everyone in the pub being out of work, as happy as they were. Some people only went for one pint. You had to look out for the locals; they were the ones that went for two pints. Two turned in to three pints; then three pints turned into a table full of empty glasses. Before you knew it, the jukebox was blasting, the newspaper is in the bin, and I'm playing pool or using the slot machine in a smoke-filled pub while everyone is dancing, hugging each other or falling over in complete hysterics. All this was happening before 2.30pm. Complete anarchy if I say so myself. By 4.30pm, once the community got a whiff of the vibes, they would arrive as fresh as a daisy to fan the flames. By 7pm while the drunks were trying to catch up to the paralytics, I was starving. It was funny and entertaining for a while, but then I would get hungry and restless. Coke and a packet of crisp could only keep me going for so long. "Mum, can I have some money to go to the shop?" Trying to interrupt a bunch of drunk people in the middle of a laughing, mumbling, swaying conversation was like trying to wake up the dead. I might as well be pulling on a tree branch; I'd probably get more of a response. "Whatttt, whattttt, what do you want some money for?" She shouted. I could tell she was annoyed. I'd be going into her beer money, but it was worth a try. Sometimes I got a pound coin to get some sweets. The gelatine gave me at least some protein. Hopefully, this was just a phase mum and dad were

going through. Half the time it was just mum and me. Dad seemed to slip away somewhere.

The time came when I was able to start my new school. Being unsettled, moving around constantly, starting the process once again messed my head up. Mum had got me into a primary school in the middle of town. Not formally a school, it looked as if it was used as a Parish. Conveniently there was a pub on the same road. Every morning mum would walk me to school. The playground, along with the classrooms all had disproportionate sizes. My class was huge. I was so far back, I could barely see the blackboard. The teacher made some effort, but I had no idea what was being taught. I just sat there because I had to, not because any of us in that class wanted to be there. The first week I had already upset the school bully. He pissed under a school table on one of our breaks, so I told the teacher, denying everything when he cornered me with his goons. That was my worst school yet. None of my time spent there had any strong points. The only events worth remembering was when I bumped heads with a girl, and a continuous nose bleed I had. I ran across the small playground, running headfirst into another girl at ten miles per hour. The lump on my head was the size of an apple. Sat in the staff room, I had to wait for mum to pick me up as I threw up in the teacher's private bathroom. There is nothing worse than banging my head; something I'm well familiar with. The second event was when my nose bled continuously

for no reason. Stood over the sink outside the makeshift toilets out on the yard, the blood just kept pouring. The teachers checked me every ten minutes. After thirty minutes, I had to be picked up to go home. If anyone went through the wars as a kid, it had to be me. During that year, there were not many kids I would consider my friend apart from Bill. Bill was my best friend who went home with his mum in the same direction as my mum and me. When it was home time, we raced through gardens, down a wall as if it was an obstacle course. I wished I could do that every day after school, but sadly mum had better ideas. When the school bell went for home time, all the parents waited by the gates. The iron gates survived the war, but the perimeter fence was cut down in the 1940s to help the war effort. Other happy parents collected their children, excited to know what their day consisted of. Mum and dad took turns to collect me. Instead of heading home for tea, we headed straight to the end of the road where a packet of crisp, and a glass of coke awaited me. Only God knows what other parents thought when I was picked up from school and taken straight into a pub. It wasn't the usual routine for a seven-year-old. Every other kid went home to a lovely meal in front of the TV. I had to sit still until mum was drunk enough to stagger home with half a lemon in her mouth, pretending it was her teeth. One was not amused. Trying to get mum home was a logistics operation. My tea was always cancelled. There was no point looking in an empty fridge. The only food I was given was a

tin of spaghetti shapes on toast, but that was only when she was sober.

The brief picture of normality would be mum and dad sat on the sofa, while I sat on the floor in front of the television. Our favourite programme came on at 7.30pm; 'The Bill.' It was a police drama about catching bad guys. 'Coronation Street' wasn't my thing; I had enough drama. After it finished, the long walk to my cold camp bed was expected, while they stayed in the warm living room by the calor gas heater. Being their only child, it would have been nice to get more affection. The only time I ever did, was when they let me lay across them on the sofa while mum played with my hair. Dad told me a joke one night when he took me to bed. He sat me on his right knee in the bedroom with just the hallway light on.

"A man and his son went through the woods looking for their dog. He had run off, and they couldn't find him. Slowly searching, they shouted his name.

"What's his name dad?"

"Erm... Jasper."

"Walking deeply through the overgrowth, there was no sign of Jasper. Getting worried, they walked for miles. I think I found something, the man said to his son. Walking behind a tree, he had found his dog. Jasper was stood on his back legs,

leaning against a tree. Hang on I'm having a piss, the dog replied."

I was in absolute stitches. Sat in the dark, we both laughed together before making him repeat the joke. Dad could be cool when he was around. My favourite, was when he used to bounce me up and down on his knee, before opening his legs leaving me to fall to the ground full of laughter. Mum was boring with never much to say. Not unless she was drunk.

When I was eight, the day of my first Holy Communion had arrived. The kids and I from my school year were all ready to receive the sacrament. The dress code was white, with an exception to the boys black pants. We all lined up outside St Wilfred's Church, the one I stole from, so this was my chance to get straight in the eyes of God. Darren shaved my head, the barber me and dad visited in town. As we walked down the aisle in single file, the priest waited to bless us at the altar. Music blurred from the organ above our heads from a balcony set away. All of our families were sat on rows of benches proudly watching. Part of the sacrament, as we all stood on stage, was to receive bread and wine. The bread was great how it stuck to the roof of my mouth. The wine, on the other hand, was disgusting. How can mum and dad drink this poison? All the parents laughed as we all pulled faces from drinking the rancid wine. Dad didn't need any more; he was still drunk from the night before. Josie from downstairs ironed his shirt for him. He missed most of it. After the

service ended, everyone headed to the building next door for refreshments. Before we dived into jelly and ice cream, all my class lined up for a photograph. Bill and I stood side by side with huge smiles showing our dimples. Everyone looked like an angel. Catherine stood out like a sore thumb. At the age of 8, she was as big as a sixteen-year-old. We had to hurry if we wanted some of the buffet. That was the happiest day of my life. All my family came to watch me; grandparents, auntie, cousins, uncle, mum and dad were all here to see me. I sat on a chair swinging my short legs eating as much as I could with a smile on my face, while my family encircled me.

Since the holy communion, everything went back to normal. Normal was not something I liked anymore. The situation started to become volatile. Money must be getting tighter because dad began to stay at home all the time. He started drinking bottles of cider with his friend 'Bluey.' Mum was now the one that wasn't seen much. They were arguing a lot; for what I didn't know. His friend now replaced mums place on the sofa for the time being during the day. 'Bluey' was a small guy with a beer belly. His black hair was hilarious. It was long on the sides but completely bold on top. He also had a beard. Being dads drinking buddy, they laughed with 3-litre bottles of cheap cider in each lap. Day after day, they did the same thing. Mum kept out of their way. It was harmless enough, but I couldn't understand why they drank

straight from the bottle instead of using a glass. They took turns going to the shop; a sad routine to say the least. This went on for a while before dad started to get violent towards mum. Half the time, I didn't pick up much being so far away in the bedroom at night, then they stopped caring if I was awake or not. Shouting, arguing, and wrestling was now the new norm. I had to hide behind the three-seater settee, while I cried in fear. Dad opened the window one night and stuck mums head out, threatening to throw her out. I panicked, not knowing what to do. All I envisioned was mum falling from the window, so I ran out of the flat, down the communal stairway and onto the street beneath the window.

"I'll catch you mum."

I soon realised there was no way I could break her fall. Just passed the pubs sat a phone box. Early hours in the morning, with dad still pushing mums head out, I ran to get help. Not knowing the number for the police, I pressed the numbers that were on the phone box pictures - 999.

"Quick, I need help. My dad is trying to push my mum out of the window."

"Where are you."

"I don't know. Near some shops and some pubs."

"Ok, well you stand on the main road, and a policeman will come and find you."

Describing the best I could, I did what the operator told me. By the time I got back, the window was open, but there was

no sign of mum. It was quiet until a green car passed. An unmarked police car with a man inside shouted me.

"Do you need help?"

Dad was arrested soon after. I went to bed while mum stayed up. I wish I could say that was the last time, but it wasn't. Three times I had to run to the phone box in the middle of the night, to call the police. Dad had a nasty side of pure violence. We had a black man that lived in the flat above us. There seemed to have been an altercation with him and my dad. One day he ran up to his flat, smashing a hammer on his door.

"Get the fuck out here now, nigger!"

He was only banging above in his flat; maybe he was moving his stuff around. It didn't take much to trigger dad off. The black man was left terrified in his flat. Chris used to tell me how my dad would go up to the biggest guy in the pub, and cause a fight or say something untoward until he was knocked out cold. What Chris didn't know was that I was in the pub watching, as my dad was sprawled on the floor, after being knocked out. His unconscious body laid under pub tables, as I tried to make sense of the silence that followed. Everyone just left him. Even my uncles acted as if this was a regular thing. Before he ended up under the table, we sat together as he drank ten pints of beer. I was the screaming four-year-old holding on to my teddy in the back of a car, as my uncles wrestled with my dad to get him in. It was sad to see infighting within my own family. It finally came to a head

when he battered mum black and blue. He broke her ribs, smashed her face in, then left her for dead. She laid outside our flat door in a pool of blood. The navy-blue carpet was stained permanently with a big circle of blood. This time dad had gone too far. He was arrested, while we were placed into a hotel by the council.

Me, Chris and mum were all together in one hotel room with three single beds. Now I know why we moved to Chorley in the first place. Feeling secure had become insecure, unsettled, and uncertain about our future. Chris hated my dad, so they always stayed apart. Everything started to make sense. I can picture what things were like way before I was born. I can imagine Chris and my dad fighting. I don't think the council or police could do much to help. Apart from being on a waiting list for a flat, we had to dwell in one room in the middle of town, not far from dads flat. How the hell could we hide from dad in the middle of town? I quite enjoyed the hotel because there was an arcade below, and we got a free breakfast. The only problem was, we didn't have a cooker. We lived on takeaways for a few months until the council found us a new home. It made no difference to me; I was lucky to get one meal a day. Mum would stay up all night waiting for a TV show that came on at 4am. 'Cell Block H' was a soap based on women in prison. I told mum to wake me up to watch it every time it came on; I loved it. Sat in our beds, we watched it together while Chris was out or asleep.

By then, Chris was well into becoming a DJ. Under his bed, he had his decks and records. When Saturday came, my Uncle Mick arrived to pick me up to go to my grandparents. It was awkward getting dressed under my bed covers, with mum and my uncle in the same room. "Who wants to look at you?" Mick would say. If only he knew what Steven did to me. I became paranoid and self-conscience after what happened. Mick had always lived with my grandparents. Being my dad's brother, I never saw my dad at their house. I don't think my dad got on well with my grandad. The cycle of drinkers seemed to continue. I didn't hate my dad. I wish he would act normal so we could be a family. All this infighting was bad for everyone.

Two months had passed, as we were getting closer to a flat offering. Sat talking, someone knocked on our hotel room door. Mum opened it to find my dad stood like the Terminator. Chris ran to the door, as all three of them wrestled to the floor. All hell had broken loose. I sat on the bed weeping for them to stop, waiting for an accident to happen. Usually, I'd cry or scream. I must be getting used to violence because it didn't phase me as much. They managed to fend him off, to the point of my dad walking away. Chris grabbed his hammer then ran up behind him down the hallway while my dad had his back turned.

"Please Chris, don't hit my dad over the head."

I begged him not to hurt my dad. Hitting him over the head would have killed him. I ran to the corridor to see what he did. Chris ran up behind him and hit him over the head with the handle. Doing so was like hitting a wasp nest with a stick. It only provoked him, and they started fighting again. The hotel staff did their best to kick him out. He kept trying to get back in over and over again, drunk and ready to attack. The receptionist stopped him a few times, but he still managed to get past when no one was around. He was like a possessed lunatic trying to kick our door in. After fending off all of his attacks, things managed to settle down again. I don't know what mum had done wrong to him, or why he was so adamant in attacking her.

Using other people's showers, living off takeaways, and sleeping in the same room, we were finally offered a flat. Thanks to dad, my new school had gone to pot. I wasn't able to go anymore for mum's safety. It seemed that every year, I had to change schools. Each time I would leave school, I had to wait for the start of a new year before I could start all over again, not learning a thing. One year on, one year off. It was pathetic. I didn't even know the alphabet. Finally, we had a home of our own; a two bedroom flat in the middle of the estate we just came from, great! The pubs and dads flat were only a few hundred yards away. Because the council owned it, mum didn't have much say as to where we lived. Given the situation, anyone would think we could change the location.

Dad was good at finding us, so I doubt it would have made a difference. I was just glad to have a home again; only this time, the three of us could start over in a good home like Chorley.

Chapter 4 - Breath of Fresh Air

I was never close to anyone from mums side of the family. Given dads track record, it's not hard to understand why they would distance themselves from me. Mum and I would visit her parents every so often. My gran seemed kind enough. My grandad on the other hand never said a word to me. He would lay on the sofa with a blanket over himself, smoking his pipe, with grey hair slicked back. The smoke-filled room suffocated my cotton clothing with his strong tobacco. At only sixty, he looked much older from the drinking and smoking throughout his life owning a pub. He was dying from liver failure and was waiting for a transplant. Mum idolised him. He was definitely her number one because it wasn't me. When it was time to leave, he wouldn't hug me. I motioned to mum, whispering by the front door.

"Why won't he cuddle me?"

"Ask him."

"No, you ask him."

"Dad will give him a cuddle."

He put his arm out with a poor effort to cuddle me. I was the bastard son of a man that beats his daughter up. I soon learnt nothing was coming to me from mums side of the family. My grandad passed away after his transplant. His body rejected the new liver. Years later my grandma was in and out of psychiatric wards. During the 1950s, she became a

victim of electric shock therapy. Back then, doctors had no idea of the effect it had on patients brains. With the voltage way higher than today's treatment, they fried her brain. It all started when she met my grandad in her late teens. She was labelled a nut-case from her outburst, so he rang the hospital, resulting in doctors with white coats on, throwing her into the back of a van and shipping her off to a psychiatric ward. If she was to be diagnosed in my day and age, I bet it would have been nothing more than a personality disorder, or bipolar at the worst. My grandad didn't think twice about having her shipped off. It was clear where mum had got her cold personality from. Mum and my Auntie Brenda took turns having her every Sunday for dinner. She would twitch a lot and played with her hands, signs of brain damage from the bastard doctors that sent high currents directly to her brain. I wish I were around at that time; I'd strap that device to the doctor's balls. It was hard work having her for the day. Taking her home was a nightmare. It's not easy driving with one hand while holding on to someone that is trying to jump out of a moving car. My mum's sister equally shared the burden. My cousin Anthony and I would visit her on our own once we were old enough. Going into mental hospitals was an adventure for two young lads. Anthony, also my age, was the only person I was ever close to from mums side of the family. They all shared a shyness about them, but my dad's impact certainly left a stain regardless of any characteristics they had. My mum inherited her dad's cold personality, while my auntie

inherited my gran's shyness. Before she became unwell, after my grandad had died, I stayed over a few times on my own. She always wore tights with a skirt. The cat she had would sit on her lap, which made me jealous. Her cat would never sit on my lap. It was entirely grey and very vicious. Hiding under a table, it hissed at me as I moved my hand closer. If I moved slow enough, it would let me stroke it, but that was rare. Most of the time it attacked me. My grandad didn't like me; I didn't imagine his cat would either.

Every Saturday at noon, I anxiously awaited for Mick to pick me. It was a world away going from a poor estate during the week, to a posh area in Fulwood at the weekends; talk about one extreme to another. My dad's side of the family loved and cared for me the best they could. It was kind of like a double-edged sword. Mick had always lived with my grandparents. I don't know why he never moved out; he had it easy I guess. My gran and granddad were both respectable people that worked hard all their life. They were upstanding pillars of the community that would bend over backwards to help people. Everyone knew them. They couldn't even go on holiday to another country without bumping into some of their friends. Our family was huge. Everyone came together on almost every occasion to share gifts, create parties, or to help each other. Nobody was left out. It turned out my gran was secretly the queen of the family. She was the one with the wisdom, organisation skills, and the person that could

make a buffet for over one hundred people within two days, right from her kitchen. Both my grandparents had many siblings so one can imagine just how big our family was. I must have had over twenty cousins, three were boys, and the rest were girls. We even had family that migrated to America, and if they weren't coming to visit us in the UK, our clan went to visit them in Sunny Florida, or on the West Coast of California. Most of this happened before I was born. It would have been great if my dad had me when he was fifteen, I would have had the chance to see it all. Mick would tell me stories as we flicked through the family photos. He would tell me about Disney in Florida, while he showed me pictures of himself stood next to Micky and Minnie Mouse. He would also tell me about their trips to Las Vegas, a tour around Alcatraz prison in San Francisco, or how lovely the bay was in San Diego. Not many people in Preston can say they went to see The Jackson 5, or Elvis Presley, live on stage. My gran's brother gave the security some money so they could walk through the back door, going straight to the front. Mick told me how he saw Michael Jackson walk right past him in a Casino. Both of them would have been children. After two or three fascinating stories, my life ambition was to move to America. Our family that lived over there were such good people. It was no surprise; how could anyone not be happy living in such a climate. Life in England is like living in the stone age compared to America. For now, I had to make do with what I had. On Arrival to their house, I would run up the garden path, making eye contact with my gran in the

kitchen as she made dinner for everyone. I ploughed through the back door and into her arms where she would pick me up for a big squeeze. She was 6ft tall and big boned with broad shoulders. Nobody would ever mess with her! Even my grandad received a few whacks whenever he drank too much whiskey. Everything had to be in order, or else.

Our oldest surviving relative was my grandad's mum, Ellen. Mick and I would visit her in her flat every week. She ate yellow haddock fish every Friday. The fish and a glass of whiskey every night must be her secret to reaching old age. When she reached ninety-eight, she had to go to a nursing home after breaking her leg. Being small and slim, she never had to carry any excess weight around. As a devoted Catholic from Ireland, she did well bringing up five kids while my great-grandad spent his time and money in the Hesketh Arms pub, while my grandad ran around in bare feet in his early years. Elderly people in her nursing home barely hung on to life, giraffe-like necks from wasted muscle while sat in god's waiting room. My great-gran was sat up having a conversation with us every time we visited. It was amazing how she was born around 1900. She lived through countless wars, including being a nurse in the first and second World War. She would have been a young child when Albert Einstein wrote his groundbreaking articles on space, time, mass and energy. I bet she had countless stories stored away in the back of her mind. One could only imagine what she

saw. She hated it when I turned up with a new haircut, short back and sides.

"Who's...who's done that? I will... I will punch their lights out. Just tell me who's done it."

She clenched her fist in front of me, with her soft-spoken Irish voice. I loved holding her shaky hands, and how her skin felt like paper. Her long nails would stab me in my palms. It was fantastic to see her reach one hundred. Queen Elizabeth II sent her a telegram. It was such an honour to get a birthday card from the Queen. Inside was a photo of Her Majesty, with a message inside.

"I am so pleased to know that you are celebrating your one-hundredth birthday. I send my congratulations and best wishes to you on such a special occasion." Signed by Her Majesty.

She peacefully passed away one week after her birthday, where she was returned to Ireland for her funeral. She was returned to the earth in her home town. Ever since, I've always wanted to live just as long, if not longer. Life itself was amazing. I wish I could live for a thousand years to see and do everything; minus becoming old and frail.

The weekends were all I focused on during the week. Monday to Friday was hell on earth with no food, nothing to do and living in a ghetto. When the weekend came, it was roast dinners sat around a table with family, cable television,

trips around the country watching football matches, and long hours out with good friends creating amazing memories. Once my five-day labour ended, it was my two-day vacation. I would give my right arm to live there full time. My gran worked in the laundry facility at the Royal Preston Hospital. She had the pleasure to meet Diana, The Princess of Wales when it first opened two years before I was born. They once owned a Spar shop and a garage with a fleet of vans that my grandad rented out, but he preferred to be a motor mechanic for the Royal Mail. Mick started window cleaning around the time I was born. He never did like anyone telling him what to do. They could have had a line of successful businesses, but I guess the working class DNA was built into them. There was no way I could live with them and look after myself. Saturday to Sunday will have to make do. It was great experiencing normal family life. Mum and dad had no interest in me whatsoever. It's a wonder how I was born. My gran was always cooking, knitting, or reading books. My grandad would relax on the sofa to catch up on his beer and whiskey, without getting too drunk. If he did my gran would kill him, let alone be late for bed when she shouted for him. I always kept Mick on his feet getting him to take me to the video shop to rent video games for my Super Nintendo. He liked renting out thrillers to watch on his bed during the day with the curtains nearly shut. We went on bike rides, raced to the shops and had play fights on the carpet like two peas in a pod. He was a big Preston North End fan. Undoubtedly, I

followed suit. We must have attended every football match, home and away.

"Shut up about bloody football."

My grandad shouted at Mick from the corner of the room, sat in his usual spot. Mick just laughed. If there were two things my grandad hated, it was football and television. His idea of relaxation was sitting in the corner with a glass of beer sat on one leg in his stone washed jeans, talking to himself or slating everyone under his breath.

"You pile of crap." "I should have never had kids." "You piece of shit."

It was pretty amusing listening to him in his element, stood on the upstairs bannister. The only annoying thing that drove Mick crazy was my grandad's tutting as he tried to get food out of his teeth with nothing more than suction.

"Will you shut up!"

Mick would finally lose it after the fifth tut as he laid on the floor watching sport. The only thing that drove me crazy was Patsy Cline every Sunday morning with my gran in full control of the record player under the stairs. Our house was inundated with visitors. There was never a dull moment.

I didn't have any friends in Fulwood until I reached seven when a boy next door knocked on for me. I stood behind my gran with curiosity when she opened the door.

"Is that boy in? Does he want to come and play?"

"Yeah go and play Joseph; this boy wants to play with you."

Stood shy at the front door, I was excited that someone asked to see me. That's when I met Daniel. He was a boy the same age as me that lived next door with foster parents. He wore a black Adidas tracksuit and had short blonde hair styled as a bob. His nickname was 'Scuddy.' You could tell this kid was cool with an attitude. I was a goody-two-shoes that couldn't tell my ass from my elbow; I knew nothing other than pubs, violence, and sex. It was great getting out. We became really good mates exploring Fulwood together. In a way, we came from similar backgrounds. Later that day he took me across the street to introduce me to another lad. Andy was an obese kid, that was obsessed with Man United. I liked him from the start. He was always hyperactive running around kicking a football pretending to be Eric Cantona, after kicking a ball into an imaginary net. Cantona was a new sensational football player that went down to be one of the all-time greats scoring 82 goals. Later, the boys introduced me to another lad named Phil, another nice lad that lived half a mile away. Every summer from that day forward was perfect. From the age of seven onwards, we stuck together like glue. It was like re-living the movie 'Stand by Me.' I played Gordie, the skinny kid. Scuddy played Chris Chambers. Andy played the chubby kid Vern, and Phil played Teddy. It was uncanny how we all fit the bill. We even had the same shaped heads. The six-week holidays were when things got really exciting.

Just across the road, we had a leisure centre. Every day we paid £1.70 to do activities such as swimming, roller disco, bouncy castle, or badminton. If we weren't running around in the leisure centre with twenty other kids, some of which being extended friends, we were in each other's house playing video games or making dens in wooded areas. Climbing was mine and scuddy's speciality; tree's, roofs, anywhere inaccessible. He wasn't as experienced as me. If it weren't for a branch that saved his fall when he landed on his balls one time, we'd have a man down. We climbed 30ft conifer trees in my grandparent's garden, high enough to see the hospital. Being so confident at climbing, I jumped straight from the top into a freefall, each branch slowly breaking my fall as I tumbled like a ragdoll. The best tree jumps had to be off a local high school roof. The tree next to the roof had long, dangly branches everyone could grab once they grew the courage to jump. If successful, it was like a bungee jump to the ground. That was the same school roof where we did a few all-nighters after sneaking out late at night. During the holidays, the caretaker lived on the school premises in a house with his dog. Scuddy and I thought it was funny to climb around the edge of the fence near his house so that his dog would chase us. It was only a sheepdog. Harmless enough, but fast as Flash Gordon. Boy, that thing could run. We found it so hilarious because the dog was always out of sight. It was only when we approached the house would it appear, running straight towards us like a greyhound chasing a rabbit. I think the dog enjoyed the

chase more than we did. All we could do was roll around on the floor laughing, trying to catch our breath on the other side of the fence. Every time the dog retreated to the other side of the house, we repeated the process. It was such a blast taunting it.

Another benefit from the six weeks holidays was mine and Micks birthday in August. Because we shared the same birthday, and practically joined at the hip, we always spent the day together. My gran would create a party for both of us every year. All my friends and cousins gathered around us with party hats on, eating sausage rolls with triangle sandwiches, while Mick and I leaned over to blow the candles out. It was a day filled with love and joy. Only God knew where mum and dad were, but I didn't care. They never attended one birthday party, let alone do anything with me. My real life was with my dad's side of the family if nothing else. How could dad be such a violent drunk when he had such a loving family. After opening all the presents, we would all go bowling, or to the cinema. I was spoilt and loved, even if it was just for the weekend. I can't imagine life without those three people. The rest of my family were great, but gran obviously pulled all the strings. She was such a selfless person. External parties were just as good from relatives, friends, or strangers. We all received an invite every week for doing everyone's buffet. After all, someone had to carry thirty trays of food into the labour club. People danced and

laughed, drank and ate, week in, week out. It was brilliant. I found it hard to include myself. Being such a shy kid, everyone tried to get me to dance, but I was happy to watch from the cushioned chairs built along the wall with a glass of coke. Some occasions, a few relatives managed to get me up to dance. I didn't know any dance moves, but I jumped and moved my arms around before shimmying off the dance floor. Inside, I wanted to let go and enjoy myself without a care in the world. The DJ stood behind his booth of flashing disco lights, taking song request every so often. It was the 90's, but with everyone's bushy hairstyles, retro clothing, and robotic dance moves, you would have thought it was the 80's.

Sunday night was always a bummer. The calm before the storm. The wealth before the strife. I knew once it got to 6pm, I was in my final hour of need before home time. I laid down on the carpet in front of the nice warm fire, with a cushion from the sofa. The Simpsons were on for precisely an hour, making my family suffer before leaving the building. After it finished, it was time to grab my stuff while Mick got his shoes on to take me back to mum. I knew there wouldn't be any food, so I grabbed loads of Pepsi and chocolate from the fridge. I didn't want to eat sugary food, but it was better than no food at all. I couldn't take anything my grandparents bought for me, because my mum had a habit of selling my

stuff in the pub for beer money. My child benefit wasn't enough for her; she had to sell what I owned.

"You don't even use it."

Mum was good at justifying things. If anyone could justify a war crime, I can guarantee, it would be her. Her outlook on life was far from dads side of the family. It made me wonder what part she played with my dad's drunken antics. Once home, I walked straight to the living room with the front door already unlocked. Mum was never about to get up to open the door in the middle of her drama on TV. I never even got a hello. I sat on the footstool covering my face with my jumper. She was transfixed to 'Heartbeat,' one of the most boring TV dramas of all time. The room was filled with tobacco smoke. Before bed, I would get hungry. It was a laugh opening the fridge door. Cheese slices and the remains of a chocolate gateau hardly constituted as food, but that's all there was. I tried to save my Pepsi and Twix chocolate bars for during the week, but most of it was gone before Monday morning. I missed countless opportunities to go on holiday to America with my grandparents. Mum always stopped me from going. She was either jealous, or she just wanted me to miss out because that's the kind of personality she had. It was like I had to pay for my dad's actions. I did, however, manage to get her permission to go to the South of France for a whole three weeks. Both uncles, my cousin, my auntie, and my grandparents took two cars to drive there and back. It was my first trip to Disney in Paris. Not what I expected from

the stories in Florida, but it was still great. The mood turned sour two days after reaching the coast from what we heard on the news. In the resort bar, everyone gathered around the television to listen to a tragedy that unfolded very close to where we had just been. My gran's idol had been in a car accident. Diana, the Princess of Wales, had been in a 90mph car crash. Shortly after she passed away. It killed the vibe for the rest of the trip. It was such a shame. Millions mourned back home, while we had to make the most of it still on holiday. We managed to get some well-earnt sun, even reaching Monaco for the day were all the rich and powerful spent their money on expensive yachts. It was a beautiful place. Green water washed up on the rocks, as we ate spaghetti pasta outside an Italian restaurant imagining what life would be like, living on a multi-million-pound vessel out in the open sea. I had come a long way from a rat-infested farm, with cow shit up to my knees. My stomach was uncommonly full of Italian food, or French Croissants. Life could certainly be amazing in the right time and place. It might as well be a dream, because like dreams, the moment will end before returning back to reality.

Chapter 5 - The Estate

"Come on Joseph, get up. We're going to view the flat."

Awaking from our hotel room that we were cramped in for weeks on end, I looked forward to having my own bedroom again. It was a short walk from town, back into the middle of the estate, a stone's throw from dads flat. I feared it wasn't the last time we saw him. On arrival, our new home was the bottom flat, in a three-storey complex that stretched halfway down the street. I imagined it was full of low-income families compacted together. As we were a family, the Council gave us the bottom flat with a big back garden, and a small front garden enclosed behind a wall with a fence. Blocks of flats surrounded us in rows and columns, with the occasional house. What stood out more, were the ten-storey-high flats that towered above us. I was glad we didn't live in one of those. When we walked in, I didn't know whether to laugh or cry. We had a large kitchen on the left with two doors leading through to the living room. At the end of the hallway was a separate toilet and bathroom. To the right, we had two bedrooms. One of us would have to sleep in the living room. I can't imagine Chris sharing a room with me. I overheard a conversation about Chris applying for a flat of his own. He had gotten a girl pregnant. I doubt mum was bothered, even though he was young. It was a smart move for most people living on the breadline. The Government will only help people with kids, so that was the trend for everyone out of

work. I liked our new home; we just had a slight problem. The flat was completely bare. The only thing installed was the kitchen worktops with a sink, as well as a bath and a toilet. The Council committed to throwing away perfectly good furniture from previous tenants. Everything we had in the past was gone. All we had were the clothes on our back, and a few bin bags filled with junk that we didn't need. We even had to go to the shop to buy lightbulbs. Anything else had to wait.

Chris conveniently vanished to find comfort elsewhere, while me and mum grinded it out for the next few weeks with nothing to even sit on. Even mum found her own comfort. Her first plan was to have a house warming. Two of her friends came around so they could have a drink in the kitchen, with worktops to sit on. Me, on the other hand, was left in the empty living room. She placed a thin bed sheet on the floor for me to lay on, while another was on top of acting as a blanket. The floor was a black marble-like stone that was as cold as the pavement outside. I shivered all night while mum got drunk in the kitchen surrounded by laughter and smoke. The first week we went without water. Our temporary toilet was a bucket that we shared. I was so cold and stiff from sleeping on that horrible floor. The third night, mum managed to get some cardboard boxes from the shop that made a hell of a difference. The ten pence crisp I lived off, was now my new bed from the empty boxes.

The weekend soon came, when Mick came to get me. Once my grandparents cottoned on, they weren't happy. They had mercy on us and bought my mum a brand new three-seater settee that pulled out into a bed. It also came with a footstool. Eventually, they ended up buying bunk beds for my room. It took a while, but gradually it felt more like home. Mum decided to paint our front door from red to yellow; her favourite colour. She took pride hanging her dad's custom-made metal plate above the front door. It looked like a registration plate that had his name 'TOME' printed in black on a yellow background. My estranged grandad's name was Tom, and everyone called him Tommy, hence the different spelling. All she did was talk about her dad, and how he could fix things in his shed, or how capable he was. To me, he was just a drunk that owned a pub who died from liver failure. She denies it of course, telling me about the time he fought with my dad, and that my dad kicked him in the liver giving him liver failure. It was a load of rubbish. He drank himself to death. It became clear why I didn't receive any affection when he was alive. I couldn't say if she drank to feel close to him, or aspired to be like him.

It soon became apparent as to what kind of people shared our neighbourhood. Stood on the wall, leaning against the fence in our small front garden, I watched the people go along with their daily lives. I had an incline from the people

we met in the pubs, but this was different. This time we were all in the thick of it. Most of the community was in exactly the same situation as us. Substance abuse, poverty, and a lack of work plagued the whole estate. I was in the metropolitan of hell. Everyone dragged each other down, and there was nothing anyone could do about it. Drunks roamed the streets like zombies. Heroin users walked in a quick march with eyes as wide as the moon, looking for an opportunity to steal. Kids begged every stranger they passed for ten pence, with the same dirty clothes they had worn all year. Without really knowing anyone, or what went on, the area seemed quiet until you noticed the obvious. Starting my new school was months away, so all I could do was hang around, again! There are only so many variations of climbing on a wall, before going back inside to an empty flat. My parents were heavy drinkers, so it's not like we ever had trouble fitting in deprived areas. We landed in paradise as far as mums concerned. I must have been the only kid with grandparents, let alone the ones I was so lucky to have. All I had to do was survive until the weekend; everyone else had to endure 365 days a year.

One fashionable night, mum took me with her to the bottom of the street so that she could have a drink with her friends. The high-rise flats were a beacon for where we lived. Having four of them erected made the population for our neighbourhood immensely high compared to the rest of the

town. One area might have a few thousand residents; we must have had over ten thousand people within one mile. Walking into the lobby, once we were buzzed through the main door, it absolutely stunk of piss. Dirty shoes had marked the floor from the hundreds of people coming and going. We pressed the elevator button for the eighth floor, two floors away from the top, and way too high for my liking. Each hallway on every level had a wall of shaped breeze blocks enabling air to flow in, and allowing people to look out over the town. The thought of falling from such a height played on my mind. Once outside the flat, her friend opened the door to let us in. Inside were two drunk Scottish men full of scars and tattoos. I knew what I was in for the second that door opened. It looked like a squatter's den. There were two manky sofas and a light bulb in the living room. Rubbish and empty beer bottles littered the carpetless floor. What a shit hole! Our flat was only a slight improvement. Mum, me, and her friend Debbie sat on one sofa, while the men sat on the other sofa, just by the side of us, as we all looked at the invisible television. All I could do was sit back covering my face with my jumper, while four cigarettes burned at the same time. I hated the smell of smoke; it was like a gas chamber. They laughed and drank having the time of their life. I wanted to throw up. How could she come down to such a low? Hours passed much slower.

"Mum, can we go now I'm hungry."

I tried to harass her to leave, but she ended up shouting at me. Then I started to beg her for money so I could go to the shop. It was never easy getting beer money out of her. My silence was bought when a pound coin was passed to me from her buddies. It was dark and late when I headed down in the lift, on my way to the shop on the lane. I don't think she was too concerned about her eight-year-old son walking to a shop at 10.45pm. The money helped me fill my pockets with crisp, chocolate and a fizzy drink. It was all in my stomach by the time I went back to the flat. There was no way I was eating in a smoke-filled room. When I got sleepy, the only option was to curl up behind mum's back, while the intoxicated sat on the edge of their seats getting rowdy. Somehow, I fell asleep with all the shouting and laughing vibrating off mums back.

A few hours went by when everyone's tone of voice had changed, waking me up instantly. Animosity quickly replaced the smoke-filled room. I woke up in fear from screams and fighting by the front door. It was two women against two, very angry Scottish blokes. The first chance I got, I made a beeline for the front door to get out. Mum and Debbie fought and wrestled on the floor with the men. No other tenants came to our aid out on the landing. It was no surprise; most of the people around us were scum to begin with. I manoeuvred towards the lift, grabbing my mums arm, dragging her towards it frightened out of my mind. One of

the Scottish men brandished a screwdriver, while Debbie and the man's friend gave their all. The lift waited for someone to step in, while I went backwards and forwards, making sure the elevator didn't go back down. Finally, I pulled mum with all my strength to get her inside while her friend was being stabbed. We reached the bottom, in what felt like the longest elevator ride of my life.

"Joseph, take the key, go home and let yourself in."

"No, just come back, I don't want to go on my own. Just leave it."

"I can't; I need to help Debbie."

"They will stab you as well."

"No they won't, just go home."

We both headed back up together, to try and save Debbie. The commotion was still going on. I kept my finger on the button, to prevent the doors from closing while my mum dragged her in. As we all headed to the ground floor, Debbie reflected on her performance, as if she had lost a round of boxing. Telling from her scars, tattoos, and now a puncture wound, she was just as bad as the men. We parted ways returning to our council-owned flats early hours in the morning. So much for a fresh start.

After that night, I completely changed my attitude towards life. It became apparent to me that this was my routine; paradise at weekends, hell on earth during the week. Giving

that the bad outweighed the good, I could feel a force. I could feel my character and personality changing to suit my surroundings. I was a good kid in a dangerous place. Becoming corrupted by my environment or ending up like these kinds of people worried me. Thanks to my grandparents who showed me the good side of life, I wasn't so easily corrupted. I was, however, lead astray, taken advantage of and super-naive. Whatever people did, I followed. I didn't know I was being neglected or starved, because I always adapted to my surroundings. I trusted the people around me to look after me. No matter how bad a situation was, people shouldn't give up or act as if the planet was about to end. I wanted to be successful and travel the world, not turn into an alcoholic or be a criminal all my life; it wasn't in my nature. Everyone accepted their destiny and gave up. That was far from my mind. My dream was to join the Army or move to America. It was sad to watch, having the opportunity to see life from both sides.

After the violent encounter, mum carried on as usual with her drinking career. She knew another alcoholic who lived on our street, but thankfully he was a nice man. Derek was a middle-aged man that lived with his dog in a ground floor flat similar to ours a few doors down. He reminded me of my dad, sat in his armchair with a bottle of cider beside him. Unlike other drunks, he was a relaxed, quiet guy. Mum enjoyed the company. He had a son my brother's age doing

time in prison. I only enjoyed going because I took a shine to his dog. Rocky was a crossbreed between a Staffordshire Bull Terrier, and an Alsatian. He wasn't a big dog, but boy did he have a mean streak in him. Over numerous visits, we created a strong bond. Derek had him since he was a puppy, carrying him home in his pocket from a pub one night. He had black and brown markings. Some dogs were all bark and no bite. Rocky was all bite and no bark. I learnt the hard way when I tried to touch his bone. Fortunately, he never bit me; a sense of trust between us shined through. While they sat on the sofa chatting away, I was on the floor rubbing Rocky's belly or playing with his floppy ears, bending them back to make him look funny.

"Can I take him for a walk, Derek?"

"No, you're not big enough to control him. He will drag you off your feet and pull you to the floor. He's never allowed off his leash."

I felt bad for him. Apart from the back yard, his only time out was to the shop with Derek to buy more cider.

The time had finally arrived when I got the opportunity. Derek took me out on the street to show me how to handle him as a trial. Rocky's lead was a robust chain-linked bit of shiny steel, attached to a leather looped handle that could go around someone's wrist. He held on to my arm, as Rocky took me for a walk. "Jeez, this dog is strong." He had more

muscle than me and probably weighed more. I had to plant my feet in the ground to gain some control. His dog was so excited to go for a walk, strangling itself against its collar. Two Rottweiler dogs walked towards us with their owner. Derek took the lead off me quick.

"If you ever see any dogs, walk in a different direction straight away."

I couldn't believe it. Rocky was trying to run towards the large dogs to attack. He was scared of nothing. Now that Derek was confident in me, I was allowed to take him to the bottom of the street and back. He jumped with excitement when I grabbed his lead, walking around my legs in circles. Smelling the floor outside, he pissed against a wall marking his territory. It made me think of the joke that my dad told me. I expected Rocky to start talking, but it never happened. I looked in his eyes, as he looked straight back at me with expectation. I know what this dog wants.

"Come on Rocky, gooooo!"

I ran towards my home ten doors away. The second I went into a sprint, he dragged me behind him, nearly pulling my arm out of its socket. The leather strap was tightly over my wrist. My slow dash turned into leaps and bounds. He was running so fast. I bounced in the air like a child pulling a balloon. We reached the bottom on the street in seconds. It was so exhilarating. When I caught my breath, we looked at each other again, repeating the run back to where we started. We stopped at mine for a few moments so that he could look

around. He walked around smelling everywhere, anxious to get back out. He was such a great dog, but very aggressive towards anyone other than Derek and me. If I hissed in his ear while pointing at someone, he would go apeshit, trying to attack them. When we walked out of my home, I forgot to put his lead on. Locking the front door, he was smelling the corner of the wall, leaving his mark like he always did. Just over my side fence was the entrance to the flats above. Rocky suddenly started growling. In a panic, I looked over to see what the problem was. There was a white Pitbull on its own growling back at Rocky. I crapped myself. Derek will go mad me if he gets injured.

"Rocky, get here now!"

Not responding to me, I didn't dare go near. All I could do was shout from over the fence. After a few seconds, they mauled each other. I had broken the fundamental rule; never let him off his lead. No dog was a match for Rocky. I wasn't worried about his safety, I just didn't want to lose him, or Derek would never trust me again. After moments of fighting out of sight, everything went calm. The white dog started walking up the street full of blood. There was no sign of Rocky.

"Shit! I hope he's not dead behind the wall."

Looking over, he was trying to catch his breath. As I looked back towards the white dog, it turned its head towards me, revealing its neck. Rocky had ripped its throat clean open.

Awestruck, I ran to put the lead back on him quick before he caused any more destruction.

"Good boyyyy."

I patted him, looking for any marks; not a scratch. I felt bad for the other dog, but the owner was a scumbag, and suddenly I wasn't at the bottom of the pecking order. Rough kids from the estate gawked at the white dog, while me and Rocky took a timeout in my garden.

"Oh my god, look at Bully's throat."

Everyone thought it was a mean dog until Rocky got hold of him. They might want to consider changing his name after that. From all the fights and battles, Rocky never lost once. I had the best fighting machine in Preston, and it's now loyal to me. I realised what I had; a new protector and a beast that would destroy anyone that would try to do me harm.

Later I found out that everyone on that estate feared Rocky. I used that as leverage with the threat of savagery whenever a gang of kids thought about taking advantage of me. Whenever they tried to bully me around a little, make fun or talk to me like I was a soft ass, I would threaten them with Rocky; the beast of all beast. The number of empty threats made me laugh. There was practically a gun in my hand.

"He's not your dog, he's Bison's, and he's in prison."

"You don't believe me? I'll go and get him."

Moments later I returned.

"He's got him as well; run!"

I bent down to Rocky's ear while unclipping his lead.

"Rocky, psssssstttt! Get em boy."

The second I hissed in his ear, every man, woman and child flocked above high ground, as my new protector frantically ran around trying to maul someone. That had to be the funniest spectacle ever; clever bastards! I knew they would run like chickens; that's why I let him loose. For the first time in my life, I felt secure.

Not bothering anyone unless they upset us, me and Rocky witnessed some pretty bad stuff together. There were times on the park when Derek, my mum, and a bunch of drunks were smashing each other's face in. We both stood on a grassy bank waiting for it to end. Derek always came off worse with cuts on his eyebrow from being punched. Preventing Rocky from protecting his owner, I stayed far away. Suddenly, violence wasn't so scary to watch, with such a loyal dog by my side. I wish we could run away forever, down a continuous road that lead to a beach. I wish he would pull me halfway around the world so that we never had to look back again. As long as we had each other, nobody on the planet could stop us from being happy.

Six months had passed, when our flat had become respectable enough for visitors. Now in comfort, we could all agree that we had finally become settled. Mum was doing her best decorating the flat, and Chris was with his pregnant girlfriend in the hostel across the road, waiting for a new flat before his baby daughter arrived. I had missed the first few months of school, so I had to wait an entire year for the following September. Boredom became imprisonment. There was nothing to do. If I wasn't climbing the front and back walls, invading resident's privacy, I was climbing the gas pipe that went all the way up from our front garden, to the third floor flat. There was a boy called Sean I befriended just over my back fence. He lived with his mum as I did. Sat with the two of them in their flat, we decided to watch a movie called Halloween. Her living room looked like something from the 70s as we watched the horror. The sun shined through the cream curtains while Michael Myers killed everyone. It was terrifying. I had nightmares for months. Every time I went, all Sean wanted to do was watch one of his Halloween movies. His bed stunk of wee. It was no wonder after watching so many horrors. Some girl from the next street would sometimes watch the movies with us. We held hands behind each other so that Sean's mum couldn't see. With everything I had already seen, it was safe to say that my childhood was gone. His mum wouldn't let him go out, which was hard to believe when she let him watch horror movies.

Being mostly alone all the time, I played football in our back garden that was in urgent need of a lawnmower. By accident, I sometimes kicked the ball over into next doors garden who shared a seven-foot fence with us. The climb was easy to retrieve it; I just couldn't be bothered, so I knocked on next door. Every time I knocked, a tall black man answered.

"Please can I have my football back?"

"Where is your football? In the garden?"

"Yes."

"OK, I'll throw it back over."

I must have kicked the ball over three times that week, and every time he answered with the same, kind response, smiling at me. He was as tall as my dad but really strong. He put his fist in front of me.

"Come on, guess which hand it's in."

"The one on the right?"

"Haha, try again."

"The one on the left?"

"Nope."

I guessed wrong three times before getting it right. His hands were massive, as I took the fifty pence from his palm. His English wasn't fluent, but he was a nice man. The next time I kicked the ball over, I did it on purpose. Not for the money, or because he was the only person I had spoken to in months. I decided to ask him something

"My mum has invited you to go for a cup of tea."

Confused, he looked down at me.

"Your mum what?"

"My mum next doorrrrr... has invited you to go for a cup of teaaaa...."

"A cup of tea?"

It was like playing Charades!

"Are you sure?"

"Yeah, she said just walk in."

I don't think his hearing was good; he had a funny walk as well. He wasn't old, but much older than my mum, and identical to Danny Glover from Lethal Weapon 4.

"Go on I'll follow you."

I stood at the front door after opening it. Mum had no idea a big black man was about to walk in. The muscles on my face twitched, as I tried to keep a straight face.

"Are you sure she said to go in?"

"Yeah sure, go straight to the end and turn left. I'm going to play football."

I bounced my ball once or twice to convince him, keeping the door open, as he walked into the unknown.

"Aaaaahhhhhh."

"Umpfff... Your Son told me that you invited me for a cup of tea."

"Joseph, get here now you little shit."

I was called a little shit often, but that was worth it. I laughed shutting the front door, staying on the front. They figured out the rest themselves.

The next time I went in, the black man was on the sofa with a cup of tea in his hand. Levi was in his late fifties and came from the Dominican Republic as part of the Windrush generation, along with his family. He came more frequently, and eventually, they got together which was my plan. I wanted her drinking to stop. Once we got to know him more, we discovered he had six sons and one daughter. His funny walk was from a car accident that nearly paralysed him. The doctors said he would never walk again, so he proved them wrong. The guy was as strong as an ox. Being a former boxer, his living room cabinet was filled with boxing trophies, mainly from some of his sons, who also took up the sport. Now we knew each other well enough; I would sometimes go next door. His youngest son, John, still lived with him. They certainly lacked in cooking skills. Each time he cooked, a large pan, with an even larger piece of meat inside boiled on the stove. The meat went between the two of them and one dog. It's not exactly the ice age, but you would think Hannibal Lecter lived next door. Dessert was the bone marrow. Even the dog shared the bone. Nothing went to

waste. They had to hang fly-catching strips from the ceiling due to the smell of the meat. Sixty dead flies were stuck to it each time. The kitchen ceiling was black with stick marks, and the wall was damaged. His son swung sticks and nunchucks around thinking he was Bruce Lee. He was really good at it as well. I loved the teenage mutant ninja turtles at the time, so it was fascinating to watch. Being the same age, Chris and John became good mates. It wasn't just the three of us anymore; we got to know Levi's family, expanding our reputation and manpower. Not all of his family took a liking to mum and me. Some of his sons were entirely against it. What we didn't know, was his ex-partner had passed away a few years prior. She was a white, Irish lady undoubtedly loved and cherished. It must have been hard losing their mum, given that she was the opposite of my mum.

It was strange having another man around. Levi lived next door, but he and his sons came to ours often. It was a whole new vibe with jokes and stories being passed around. We all seemed pretty happy as the summer months brought some excellent sunshine. In my room was a small ghetto blaster that played cassette tapes. It was the era of a new kind of music called 'Jungle' that later became known as drum and bass. Chris was well into his Djing even playing in nightclubs. Pushed wide open, I would blast my Jungle tapes out of my window to impress him as he walked across the road from his hostel. We blocked a lot of bad stuff out with

water fights on the front creating memories. No matter how hard we tried, there was always something bad waiting to happen. During his time at the hostel, there was a woman that became verbally abusive to Chris's girlfriend. Once he found out, he walked into her room going mad, warning her to stay away. Later she committed suicide. It wasn't his fault, the woman had mental problems, and the confrontation tipped her over the edge. Most people had some problem where we lived.

When things seemed to be improving, a few months after settling in, my lunatic of a dad had found out where we lived. Marching hell-bent towards me down our street, I ran in to sound the alarm. He walked straight through the front door in the hunt for mum. Chris and John did their best to push him out, before ending up on the floor. Thinking it was all over, he came back with a screwdriver. Watching from the end of the corridor, they wrestled on the ground once again until they grappled the weapon off him. Mum hid in the living room while the three men wrestled. Dad could have found out about Levi. After repelling the attack, that was the last time I saw dad for a long time. I believe my gran had finally got through to him. He booked himself into an alcoholic rehab for six months in Blackpool. His drink-drug cocktail fuelled him into Jekyll and Hyde. At last, he admitted he had a problem. Being in pubs from the age of fourteen, it was bound to catch up with him. My

grandparents and I went to visit him from time to time. How he never ended up in prison was beyond me. Mum had a newspaper cut-out from a time he was arrested.

"A man was arrested after refusing to leave the Royal Preston Hospital. Peter, who was asleep on one of the hospital beds, after a drink-drug cocktail, dismissed the hospital staff when they told him to leave. When the police arrived, Peter replied saying: come in here, and I'll make mincemeat out of you."

That was my dad all right; a real nutter. He met his match one time in the town centre when four police officers kicked the shit out of him for being drunk and uncooperative. My Uncle Mick went mad. It wasn't right what they did to him, but dad could definitely start trouble, even if he never finished it. What pissed me off the most, was how he moved away once he became sober. Bournemouth was nearly three hundred miles down south, on the coast. Supposedly, it was a place where he, and my uncles spent their summer vacations as kids. What was the point? I'd never see him again. The fact was, he abandoned me.

Seeing more happier days, mum, Chris, and his cousin had a few drinks one night, as everyone listened to music in our half-furnished flat. The lady in the flat above us lived on her own, so my mum invited her to join us for a few hours. Not yet carpeted, the floor was black with the marble-like surface I had slept on. Not much of a drinker, the lady just smoked cannabis. Everyone had fun until she lost it.

"Where is it? My weed has gone."

Becoming more agitated, the woman started to get paranoid.

"Have you got it? It's not just disappeared."

Blaming my brother and his cousin, she increasingly became more volatile. Aiming her attention to his cousin, he was blamed for stealing it.

"I've not touched your weed; I don't even smoke it."

Frantically walking around the flat trying to find it, no one could see it anywhere. Stood under the bedroom doorway, she pulled a knife out and stabbed my brother's cousin deep in his stomach, before leaving the flat. Shouts and panic bellowed from our windows.

"Levi quick, get him in the car."

Falling limp, Chris and Levi carried him to the car. Levi drove at eighty miles per hour through red traffic lights before he nearly died.

"Hold on lad; don't go to sleep."

"We are nearly there; just hang on."

Having been stabbed in the stomach, he bled and bled internally, giving him much needed time for anyone to save him. If he were stabbed in his vital organs, it would have been over in a minute.

"Quick, someone get me a doctor."

Rushing out, nurses and doctors rushed him to surgery just as his luck had nearly run out. Being the good guy he was, he didn't deserve to die. He luckily made a full recovery. The woman that stabbed him avoided jail because she was six months pregnant.

Two of Chris's friends were not so lucky on that estate. One of them stabbed a black man to death after stealing his shoes worth £120 from his flat. The other stabbed a man to death for disrespecting his girlfriend. Each of them received life in prison for premeditated murder. Fifteen years in jail was a scary thought, even if it was cut down to ten for good behaviour. I didn't know one person with rationality from that estate. Chris also had a friend that was given life in prison for holding his dying friend after being stabbed. It was not a good environment to grow up in, but that's just how it was.

Levi and mum became close over time. He was a cool guy. His family didn't like the fact that he was moving on, but he just wanted to be happy. Nobody could see that. His family had tough skin. Some were borderline gangsters. Half of his family seemed intimidating. The other half made an effort in getting to know us. Now more of a stepdad, some of his sons thought he was spending more time with me, instead of his grandkids. All we ever did was go to the shop in his car. Levi was a laid-back guy. I wouldn't say he ever spent quality time

with me; it was mainly about him and my mum. That didn't stop one of his sons from reaching across the driver's side, to try and grab me. Levi pulled up outside his son's house to see if they were ok one day. I was pretty scared of his family. On the other hand, they deterred anyone from bothering us. Everyone in Preston knew them in a friendly way, I mean let's face it, who would ever stand up to an ex-boxer that was built like a brick shithouse, with an army of sons ready to take the world on. My mum got away with murder. Just when I thought he might calm her down, she used him for his money to drink every day and to cause havoc. It was like a license to steal. Every pub we crawled to, she would cause loads of trouble, then hide behind poor Levi whenever the shit hit the fan. I felt really bad for him. He wasn't the brightest book on the shelf but always had good intentions. Mum needed sorting out. I just wanted the madness to stop. We needed good stability in a shit situation. After my abuse on the farm, I thought she would experience a wake-up call. Nothing changed the way she was, and so it went on drinking into oblivion. She was the fire, while Levi was the petrol fuelling the insanity. I hated how she flaunted around like everything was a big joke. She was the star of her show, while the rest of us were her chaperones.

Levi continued to live next door, with plans to move in with us. There was no point in having two flats next door to each other. He received compensation for his back, as well as

receiving disability benefits. I only know because she spent it, and it was the only time she bought some clothes for Chris and me. He wasn't far from his pension after spending his life in the motor trade like my family. My mum took full advantage of him. She didn't care about anyone but herself. Cracks began to surface into her true nature. It was pathetic listening to her tell Levi stories, while drunk. He was taken in by everything she said. Bullshit stories about her dad, or how she climbed Ben Nevis and jumped out of a plane at 10,000 feet. All of which, I found questionable. She became a drunk like her dad, that's the only story she can tell. I was starting to lose my patience with her. She finally met her match when she became toxic towards Levi and me. One night at home while drunk on her high horse, she started kicking off, keeping us both up all night. It got to a point where she kicked Levi and me out of the flat. I wasn't initially kicked out. She climbed into my bunk bed, leaving me with nowhere to sleep. Only having one mattress, she had fallen asleep in my bed, while we had no choice but to stay next door. I ended up sleeping on John's bed, while he played on his PC. Poor Levi sat in his living room in the dark. The next day his daughter came around to ask us what happened. She was furious like a storm. Mum just pissed off the wrong family. His daughter marched straight into my bedroom, climbed my bunk bed and punched the shit out her. We didn't witness it, but her whole arms were black and blue from covering her face. When I returned home, I found her cowering in the corner on my top bunk. It was sad that it

came to this. At the same time, she brought it on herself. She was able to put me through hell, but the second she did it to someone else, she got knocked down a level or two. Being so young, I didn't have a voice. I was shocked by how Levi defended anything she did wrong towards me. She never let it drop, about how his daughter kicked the shit out of her. From that day forward, she had him right where she wanted.

The last piece of the puzzle, to how life worked on the estate, finally came together when I started my new primary school in the next street. I endured the longest boredom of my entire life; it couldn't come fast enough. At least I could look forward to free school dinners with something to do during the day. At the age of ten, my school attendance had become ridiculous since leaving nursery. I was in the last year before high school, and not prepared one bit. I had no education thanks to mum and dad. The exams took place at the end of the year before we broke up for the summer holidays. There was no way I could learn five years worth of education to get any questions right. My first day felt great in my new uniform. Mum hated it when I changed schools. Buying new uniforms cost her a small fortune. All she did was complain. I had already looked around the school a few months prior, so I knew where the entrance was. The first morning, my name was shouted to wake me up from the opposite bedroom; that was about as much enthusiasm as mum gave. My new school seemed the best so far. The layout was cool,

the teachers were friendly, and the dinners were delicious. Our headmistress was a lovely lady who showed off her piano skills with an opera singing voice. The kids in my class weren't all bad, apart from a few off the estate that I didn't know yet. The teacher sat me next to a round table with other kids. A mixed-race girl was naughty, repeatedly asking to go to the toilet. You could tell she was local. She started verbally shouting at the teacher, before telling her to fuck off on her way out, slamming the door shut. I couldn't believe it, at the same time it had to be expected. One of the bad boys started whispering to me.

"Oi you, what's your name?"

I faced the teacher ignoring him. I later found out when he was in a fight with another kid from the estate, that he was the cock of the school. Regardless, it was still a pleasant environment. Integrating went smooth once they all found out who I was.

Every Thursday, we lined up on the yard to get on the bus that took us swimming. The boy's raced to the back of the bus to get the back seats. There was only one time I raced because I was already at the front of the queue. Running down the bus aisle, just as I was about the reach the back step, one of the lads had tripped me up. By accident or not, I smashed the side of my nose against the back step. By the time I stood up crying, all the kids were in their seats. Blood gushed from a large cut down the side of my nostril. Within

seconds, I stood in a pool of blood before the teachers took me to the staff room to wait for an ambulance. The hole went straight through. Shaking from all the blood loss, I drank five glasses of water from thirst, like I'd been on a desert island for a week. It seemed like a major accident would happen after every change in my life.

After some time, a whole network of people, and the goings on throughout the estate revealed itself. There was always something happening such as a crime or a drama, that always took the edge off any nerves. Awkward silence made me feel uncomfortable. I never intended to be bad or to get involved with those people. I suddenly found myself being a street kid, seeing the same faces every day. The environment becomes a tide. If we didn't go with the flow, we would get washed away. Everything becomes strange. The daily experiences mixed with everyone's unique personality became second nature. It seemed like every moment was meant to happen. Any differences that didn't follow suit became greyed out. The same thing happened in Chorley. That's when I knew I had to go with it. The transition left me disheartened of course, when I was attacked three times and punched in the face from evil kids, while I cried on the floor. Violence terrified me. Nobody knew what I witnessed with my dad and my mum's ex-boyfriends. They thought I was the biggest pussy ever. To me, violence horrified me. At the age of ten, I believe I had something similar to PTSD, but who

knew or cared. "Sort yourself out" was the antidote that everyone used. Mental health problems were laughed at. It didn't matter if I woke up screaming with nightmares about violence. It didn't matter if I shook uncontrollably every time two people argued, or if I ran away every time there was a loud bang. My peers took me for a weak, skinny loser. They were right. I weighed no more than three bags of sugar, and was terrified of my own shadow; literally. Everyone gave me a pass thanks to my stepdad and his family, as well as Chris and his reputation. That acceptance gave me enough time to adapt to my surroundings, something I was brilliant at.

"Go on Joseph, hit him!"

"He's a free target, just hit him!"

"Come on."

I punched and punched until my arms became tired. There was a tramp in my class that everyone hated. He always stunk of piss and shit. I don't know if he did it on purpose for everyone to leave him alone, but boy did he smell. Now in a gang, hanging around with the cock of the school among others, I was expected to do what they did. Everyone hated the tramp. He had a rat face, rat hair and stunk. I didn't want to hit him. The whole situation was made out to be fun. The poor guy was bullied every day, but no wonder. He just grinned, making it worse for himself. He looked me in my eyes as I punched away, while my gang had hold of him on

each side. He knew I was the weak link in the chain. After a few weeks, he followed me home, insisting he was going to get me. I laughed at him, occasionally turning around to look as he trailed me. I wasn't trailing him with his smell, that was for sure. Out of the blue, he ran up from behind and punched me hard in the nose. I stood crying while the blood pissed out. He got me from behind as revenge. It was my own fault of course, but expectations were in place. My quality of life wouldn't be smooth if I didn't meet those expectations. Ever since, I had a kind of resentment that slowly built up. Corruption shook me to the core, as it naturally would to a child. The innocence gradually left me in semesters. Bad influence embalmed me every day. I knew it was wrong, yet I embraced it because I had to. I bullied and battered that tramp for the rest of the year, calling him every name under the sun. As the saying goes; if you can't beat them, join them. It was dog-eat-dog as Rocky taught me.

Come 5pm, while everyone drove home from work leading a normal life, thirty kids were congregating around the shops getting ready to terrorise the community. Within the ranks were four generations of gang members. First, there were the young kids that would throw stones, attack you for no reason, or swear at you; kind of like ankle-biting dogs. Then there was my age group, ten to thirteen-year-olds that owned the streets far and wide, stealing and terrorising. After that, was Chris's age group with people in their early twenties

dealing drugs, committing murder, having parties galore, and shagging every woman in sight. Finally, there were seasoned criminals aged forty that had spent hard time in prison, smoked and drank their fair share of substances, while hanging around pubs all day creating a name for themselves. I'd say there were five generations, but the elders were inactive, barely hanging on to life. They would go down with the ship holding on to their way of life until the end. It all started when grandparents and parents left their kids astray, creating an eternal cycle of shit, day in, day out. People labelled us a gang; it's more like a community or a family brought together from the same social situation. Nobody goes out of their way to live like we did, its imposed upon us. I was slap-bang in the middle of that cycle of hell. Each member had their own unique traits, and what a freak show. With the right conditions, at the right time, society can spew out an epitome of exactly what's wrong with this country. Here are some examples in no particular order.

- There was a boxer that wanted to fight everyone and usually lead us into armed riots. (Leader)
- Thieves that stole from their own family, the public, or shops in town.
- Jokers that set fire to buildings, bins, and cars, or threw fireworks into shops.
- Evil who would find pleasure from terrorising old or vulnerable people.

- The perverted who would start wanking in the middle of the street, or pull everyone's pants down for a laugh.
- Opportunist that would assault, steal, or abuse in situations they could take advantage of.
- A supplier that supplied everyone's drink and drugs, as well as locating parties to crash, girls to take advantage of, or homes to burgle.
- A racist that would assault and attack groups from ethnic minorities.
- Thrill seekers that would steal busses, tractors, motorbikes, cars, etc.
- A terroriser that would smash up everything, including police cars.
- Scruffy kids known to be lookouts and beggars.

Some individuals had a few or all of these traits. Being together in a group, we took advantage of every single opportunity that presented itself day and night. It was pure madness. Sadly, their behaviour started from a very young age, barely scratching the surface. A Child psychologist would have a field day. Then last, but not least you had me; someone that loved being chased by citizens or the police. I wasn't a hardened criminal, or confident to do serious crimes, but I could certainly run, or do crazy stunts on motorbikes. Just like school, I wasn't there from the beginning. Being at the bottom of the pecking order, I might

have been in the gang, but still wasn't thought of enough to be given a task. Members wouldn't teach me how to hotwire a car, or how to roll a joint. That was my blessing in disguise. The less I knew, the better the outcome I'd have. Like a dog chasing a stick, I didn't know what to do once I caught it. With all the bad stuff, I still fought hard to stay good. Each one of us had the same shitty parents, that spent all the money in the pub. Some families were good, but flat broke in poverty. They had no idea what their kids were getting up to, nor did they care enough to ask. Even the police couldn't handle us. Whenever they answered a call, they would return to a police car with smashed windows, flat tyres, and graffiti written all over in spray paint. Watching eight police officers in five vehicles, trying to catch twenty of us, beats watching television any day. When it got on-top (hot) we set alight bins in the middle of the road creating a blockade. Being built, I believe in the 1950s, we had a network of inaccessible pathways, fences to climb over, or homes we could camp in until the coast was clear. Every time I returned home, I'd be panting in front of my silent mother that was transfixed to some crap on television. She would focus on rolling a cigarette for a second with her elbows on her knees before whispering concerning words.

"What have you been doing then?"

She didn't give a monkey's. That was her slow, lethargic automated response without eye contact. I could have told her I had murdered someone. It would have fallen on deaf

ears. The total ignorance around me gave me an incentive never to cross the line. To become like those around me was unthinkable. While everyone was going into peril, I knew if I crossed that line, there was no coming back. All I wanted to do was see Mickey Mouse in Florida.

Trembling in my bedroom, my heart was beating hard as I tied my shoelaces. The feeling became more regular, every time I got ready to go out. Anxiety filled my system as the adrenaline pumped around my body. Blood was pushed to my vital organs to function better, leaving my hands and feet freezing cold.

"I'm going out mum."

I didn't have a flight or fight response; just a flight response. The second I got outside I sprinted towards the heart of the action, bursting vast amounts of energy to where everyone congregated. I was a rabbit that avoided capture, and I loved every second of it. Fear turned into adrenaline that became a rush like a drug that I needed every day.

I lived for the chase until I finally met my match. In a small group of four, we flocked in the middle of the road running West holding stones. Uninformed until the last minute, the plan was to throw stones at a window on the third floor. Direct hit! One of us, certainly not my left hand, directly smashed it. No one came out of the flat; it seemed empty. An

hour or so passed when it finally kicked off like a slow releasing drug.

"It's Iron Man, run!"

"Who the hell is Iron Man?"

A topless man charged directly towards us with hate-filled eyes. I wish I knew earlier why they called him Iron Man because this guy was a muscle-bound lunatic, that chased us for three straight days. At first, it was funny because we were too fast and agile for him. He climbed every fence we did and scaled every wall. We were on red alert. No one came out unless they needed to. Not unless they were ready to be chased for an hour. The third day, some of the lads stole a motorbike, trying to get back to normality. Iron Man had really screwed up our routine. Stood by the garages, we attempted to hotwire it while everything seemed calm. Razzing past us on a push bike, a lookout informed us of some bad news.

"Quick, Iron Man's coming!"

"Kane, get in the garage quick," Lee shouted.

"I'm sick of running. I've not even done anything."

The boys hid in the garage with the motorbike, locking themselves in. I stood at the end of the garages, just by the road. It was like a Western movie. He would be at one end, while I was at the other. Prepared with nothing but a lie, Clint Eastwood would have been proud standing my ground. I don't know when I turned into a diplomat. Who was I to

think this guy had any rationality. I hated being called a pussy. It was an opportunity to climb the ranks. The meaning of a man's life comes down to just one action. Before I realised the saying referred to men, not boys, he appeared from around the corner. Eyes wide open, bouncing muscles, and still topless, he charged straight at me. I concluded there was no way we could find an amicable solution when his golf ball flew past my head. I curled up in a bowl on the floor, begging for mercy. So much for valiance.

"It wasn't me, I swear."

He roughed me up a little, before dragging me down the street backwards by the scruff of my neck. My jumper strangled me; it was terrifying. I couldn't breathe at all, choking on my own tongue, squealing like a pig. It was too tight around my neck to get my fingers in. My own weight nearly choked me to death as my ankles were dragged along the floor.

"I'm taking you back to my flat; I'm going to tie you up, then kick the shit out of you for three days, after making me chase you for three days."

He displayed me for the whole community to see. The sister of our gang leader who whispered to me on my first day at school ran over and wrestled with him.

"Get off him now!"

"No, he's fucking coming with me!"

"John, Mark, Allen, get here now and help me."

She was looking over her shoulder shouting imaginary names, to get him to release me. In fear of reprisal, he gave up his catch and dropped me to the floor before walking off. Thank god someone came to my rescue before we reached his flat. I thought I'd never live long enough to see high school. From that day on, I stuck to what I knew; Running! I went home to brush myself off. Things like that never deterred us. We owned the streets. I could have had his home petrol bombed, his legs broke, then chased out of the estate if I wanted. We certainly had the resources, manpower, and willingness. The art of crime was getting away with it. To me, it was just part and parcel. Being bad was far too alien for me. The love from my grandparents always came back to haunt me, that's why I never crossed the line into serious crime.

Food was always hard to come by for some of us. It didn't matter how scummy some parents were, they still managed to put food on the table, and that really pissed me off. The only time I questioned my mum's responsibility was when I watched kids begging on the streets for ten pence, while others got a guaranteed meal after school. Butter, maybe some cheese slices, and rock-hard bread seemed like an endless choice. Occasionally, my friends would make some toast for me at their house. I'd never seen two loaves of bread before next to each other. Even mums friends sometimes made me a meal. They knew she wasn't looking after me. I

became that skinny; I looked anorexic in some of the family photographs. I ripped them up with embarrassment. Living at home was like a concentration camp, but cleaner. I believe that's why our gang became close to one another; each one of our parents was drinking in the pub. After galavanting around Preston, we always went for a pit stop, and a game of pool while our mums and dads propped each other up. The hope was to get a few quid out of them to be able to get some chips. Not once could we afford a burger from a takeaway with the money they gave us. They had to be drunk enough to hand over the money, but not too drunk, or the money would be gone. The timing was important. They were the shit; we were the flies. Some kids took a gamble on the slot machine, to try and turn £1 into £15. We walked around looking at the pub floor for loose change. Levi just sat at home, went to the bookies, or sat quietly next to my mum with a glass of lemonade. The well-known respected man, now had a little devil on his shoulder, whispering evil deeds into his ear while she marvelled in power. He listened and stuck by her as she tightened her grip on him like a snake. I started to see beyond her motherhood, and all I could see was a fraud, a woman that poisoned everything she touched. After my campaign of starvation without one complaint, I decided to put my foot down. Chris went mad at her in the past for empty cupboards; maybe it was time I stood up to her.

"Mum I'm starving, and there is never any food in."

"I've no money, Levi will you tell him."

"Don't get me involved; that's between you and your son."

"I want some food now, or I'm ringing the police."

"I'll get some tomorrow; will you shut up I can't hear the telly."

"You won't though; you never do because you spend it on fags and beer."

I stormed out to the nearest phone box. It was the same phone box I used when my dad was sticking her head out of the window, and this is the thanks I get. Maybe I should have let him, I thought to myself. As I explained to the operator how my mum wasn't feeding me, Levi pulled up in his car.

"Joseph, put the phone down will you. I'll go to the shop and get some bread."

"Bread? I don't want bread; I want a meal." His answer insulted me.

"I promise tomorrow I will get you some food."

I put the phone down for his effort. At least he was trying. My mum did nothing for me. I wanted to eat a nice warm meal that every child was entitled to, like some of my friends. I was so angry with her. She only cared about the drink. I wish I could say things changed after that, but they never did. School dinners, along with my grans cooking had to make do. With all my running every night playing cat and

mouse, I burnt loads of calories off, not that I knew what calories were.

The school year was over when my exam date finally approached. Being the youngest in my year, I'd still be eleven by the time I started high school. We all had plenty of time to prepare for the final test. "Try your best," the teachers kept telling me. Unless I can rewind five years of education, there was no hope for me. They placed us in the main hall, with desk and chairs equally spaced out. I didn't see what the fuss was. The results determined which set we were placed in. That's when the penny dropped. Set one was the highest for the smart kids, while set four was the lowest for the dumb kids that misbehaved. I looked around at the sea of heads looking down on their papers. The questions might as well be in Chinese. Screw it! Tick, tick, tick, tick, done! My guess was as good as any because that's all I did. I wish everyone would hurry up so I could go home. Thirty minutes passed with a feeling of dread. I failed miserably. Miraculously, I was placed in set three for maths. There was no equation to it really, I just randomly ticked away. The six weeks holidays kicked in before moving up to the big school. The fear never concerned me, until that first day arrived.

I felt great whenever I put a new uniform on. Levi showed me how to do my tie, along with John. I wish my dad could see me. On my first day, mum paraded me outside our flat

while eagerly waiting for us both to set off on my new adventure. She leaned towards me, pointing down the street.

"School is that way."

"Are you not even taking me? It's my first day."

"There is a boy there from the same school; go with him."

"I don't even know him."

"You will make friends."

"Why can't you just come?"

"I can't; I have things to do."

Words failed me. I walked off astounded. Basically, it's too far, and she can't be bothered. It wasn't the safest routes, walking through a mile of wooded surroundings at 8am. Other kids walked in groups, so I followed them. I didn't even know where it was. The following year, a six-year-old Muslim boy was raped and murdered on my same path to school, so it felt like a minefield. The police eventually caught the killer, but it wasn't during my time at that school. I could have been that boy. It was a black man from the high-rise flats we lived near.

Once getting over the first few days, school seemed fun. Most kids from the estate attended, so we took over in no time. The cock of the school was our gang leader unsurprisingly. Everyone soon knew their place. The other lads we met were from the surrounding areas, and now our gang had become

an army. We didn't have to worry about bigger lads from the last year, they were just an older generation from our estate, about to leave into a life of crime instead of employment. I met some great friends. Not one person came from the kind of background we did. We were a force to be reckoned with. It amused me how normal lads hung around us, curious at what kind of people we were. The rest of Preston must be average compared to us. Not many kids went to prison before reaching high school. We were in a league of our own. At the same time, it felt great being part of something we controlled. My class each day was a total zoo. Nobody could hear the teacher. Missiles were launched around the room. Teachers screamed until their eyes popped out. Home life was that bad, school became a place to let my hair down. I ran wild with the rest of the class, having the best time of my life. My behaviour was picked up, resulting in detentions all the time with the headmaster. When the bell went at dinner time, those on detention were expected to go right away. After it finished, we had ten minutes to get some food from the cafeteria before next class. By the time we got there, we had nothing but scraps; it was torture. Receiving no food from home, those dinners were my lifeline. Once that bell went, instead of going to detention, I ran to the dinner hall to get the first choice. I planned to eat my food in five minutes, then run straight to detention hoping the headmaster wouldn't click on. Of course, he did, each time adding more detentions. I pulled it off a few times without him knowing. All the bad kids from the entire school looked at me, while I

did the walk of shame with a stomach full of food, or with fresh sandwiches and flapjacks in my bag. It was delicious, to say the least. Metal trays were lined with pizza, garlic bread, and chips. No consequences in the world were keeping me away from that food. It was all I received in twenty-four hours; I even stole some to take home. That's the only reason I went to school in the first place. Half the time I nicked off with my friends and went to town window shopping. School was also a place where I could distance myself from the estate and the gang. That area along with the people didn't reflect who I was as a person.

Once familiarising myself with everyone, I had fallen for the hottest girl in the school. Being two years above me, she hung around with my gang leader's sister; the girl that saved me from being strangled to death by Iron Man. I was the last person she would get with. She had a crush on our leader, but he wasn't interested. That didn't stop her giving me messages to deliver to him, knowing how close I was to him. Still frigid, I'd never kissed a girl. Her long blonde hair went to her bum and had a face carved from angels. She knew I fancied her because I made it clear. When the whole school is friends with each other, inside and outside of school, its different from having a simple crush on someone. We ended up talking whenever we passed in the hallway. She always smiled at me, knowing full well I was in love. She thought it was cute. Having started puberty, I was already

masturbating every night. My emotions were all over the place. After sending messages to her through my friends and hers, she finally got the message. Taking it one step further than most boys that chased her, I flirted and spoke to her every chance I got. She started giving me hugs which were a big thing for most lads in the first year. Having her full attention, nothing stopped me from lynching her in the corridor. Every time we passed, we walked towards each other with open arms, before kissing each other; it was pure bliss. Typically, a skinny eleven-year-old, years below would never get the chance I got. Because I was known, had respect, and the confidence to do crazy shit, I was able to get plenty of groping and kissing from the hottest girl during toilet breaks. All my friends were jealous.

"Check this out lads; Joseph thinks he's got in with the hottest girl of the school three years above."

"He's lying. Why would a year ten girl kiss you, you're not even twelve yet."

"Don't believe me? Watch this then."

I put my arms around her then kissed her, turned around and gave a cheeky smile with my large dimples to my new friends. They thought I was lucky, but luck had nothing to do with it. Back on the streets, if we wanted something, we took it; and she was the only thing I wanted. She smoked and did as many detentions as I did, so she was a bit of a bad girl. Nothing ever came from it. I was punched in the jaw a year later by a Muslim gang member when I turned my head

away. Unknown to my knowledge, he had a thing for her or maybe something more. Another coward to punch me when I had my back turned. I wasn't known for fighting. It didn't make sense for boys to blindside me. Then I would remember rule number one; always attack when they least expect it. Maybe some girls are not worth the trouble, so I left her be. By that time I already had three girlfriends, so it wasn't like I was in short supply. One would leave my house, as another would come. I gained plenty of sexual experience before losing my virginity at fourteen. My parents might be a waste of space, but I can't thank them enough for giving me good looks and common sense. I had any girl I wanted, and seeing as I was a lover, not a fighter, it was a done deal.

During times of no detention, my spare time was filled roaming around the corridors, seeing and learning what everyone else was doing. Whereas everyone had their little groups, I didn't belong anywhere. There was always a fear inside me of missing out on something. I'd joke or spend time with some friends, before moving on to another group. Some kids smoked, played football, had fights, told jokes, while other geeks harassed teachers outside the staff room. Before starting that school, I could count all my friends on one hand; now I had over one hundred. Two particular good friends were the ones that always got me in trouble. One laughed at me from behind the teachers back, while I was getting shouted out, then vice versa, I'd laugh at him while

he was getting in trouble. It was brilliant. During the woodwork class one afternoon, our antics took a twist when we both started to screw around. Chasing my best friend Chris around a square table filled with mounted vices, my tall, bald teacher was getting very impatient.

"Stop running now!"

Being that I was the pursuer, he quickly turned his attention to me. Not listening to a word the teacher said, we continued. On my third lap, he grabbed a hand full of my tie and jumper, picked me up above his head, and slapped me hard across my neck before letting go. I couldn't believe it. The whole class was awestruck. Teachers weren't allowed to hit us. Once my feet touched the ground, I ran out of school through the dangerous forest, and back home. Even my mum was in shock.

"Levi, the fucking teacher just hit him."

"What! I'm going to kill him. Pass me my walking stick. I'm going down in the car to knock his fucking head off, see how he likes it."

I persuaded them not to go. Instead, they made a few phone calls to the school. The bastard should've been arrested, but lost his job instead. My neck was red with a huge handprint. Physical discipline ended shortly after being born, yet I've been thrown through doors, now slapped across the face. I always did have a cheeky smile. Levi and his family were ready to kill him. Strangely enough, his daughter had

punched the deputy female teacher when she attended that school, many years prior. The apple doesn't fall far from the tree.

From most of the classes I attended throughout the day, the same faces joined me at the bottom of the pile. Paul, who became a good friend, lived a very similar kind of life as me. His mum frequently drank, while he and his siblings lived off toast like me. It was good knowing I wasn't alone. Living just over a mile away, his house was historically old on a lane that once homed the Mill Workers in the 1800s. Each time I visited, he and his family told me stories about how their house was haunted. They shared stories about how they would wake up in the morning to find photo frames off the wall, then left in a straight line on the floor. Objects in the kitchen would move before their eyes. Telling me with a real sense of conviction, I knew when someone was lying. His whole family shared their different experiences, and how they had to avoid certain rooms or act in certain ways in order not to upset the spirit. Being scared as they told me, his mum was on medication from the bad experiences she had witnessed. They were too poor to move house. Frequenting his house very often, I ended up having a sleepover. After hearing the stories, I became reluctant to stay. His mum was out for the night, leaving me and Paul, his two younger brothers, and his older sister to do what we wanted. The sleeping arrangements had Paul with his

brothers in his mum's room. That was the only room with no paranormal activity. I was in the next big room with his sister. Letting me stay in her bed, she slept on the floor in a sleeping bag just beside me. When it came to bedtime, his sister and I got into our sleeping positions. With the ceiling light on, Paul and his brothers messed around in the kitchen eating toast. Getting impatient, his sister climbed out of her sleeping bag and headed downstairs to drag the trio to bed.

"I'm going to kill them."

Lying on her single bed with my hands behind my head, I looked up at the ceiling bulb or around the room, with a tense feeling from all the ghost stories they told me. The large room was pretty empty, being so poor. Other than a bulb and a single bed, it was a familiar sight in poor households. Her bedroom door was wide open, as I could just about hear the four of them squabble downstairs. The big old empty house made my skin crawl. I wish they would hurry up, I thought. Looking around the room, it suddenly went really cold, so I moved my arms from behind my head, then put them under the cover. Looking on to the landing, out of nowhere her bedroom door that was wide open just slammed shut. Terrified, I threw the bed cover over my head shaking like a leaf. The loud bang made me jump as I watched it close faster than any human could. There was no draft, and even if there was, the door was wide open in her room. No draft in the world could've got behind it. The light from the ceiling bulb shined through my duvet, while I froze

keeping my eyes wide open. Patiently waiting, I prayed for his sister to come back. Ten minutes of silence drove fear into me before she finally walked into the room.

"What was that bang?"

"The door just slammed; I want to go home."

She calmed me down, reassuring me nothing else would happen. I was looking right at the door when it happened; there was no string attached to the handle, and from her expression, she seemed as shocked as me, promising that it wasn't a prank. The four of them swore blind that it wasn't a prank, even years later. The door opened into his sister's room. The speed of how it slammed was frightful. I'd never seen an object move so fast in my life. Not really believing in ghost before that night, the spirit was described as jealous. No wonder his mum was a nervous wreck. That was my first and last night sleeping in that house. The experience will stay with me forever. Twice, the priest came to perform a blessing with no avail. Eventually, they moved out.

My fun ended by the time I had reached year nine. Just over two years at my new school, with teachers trying to get through to me, I couldn't calm down. There was no way detention came before food; I was too hungry. Being suspended twice already for misbehaviour, the headmaster called me into his office for a meeting. My mum and grandparents sat around me, while my white-haired Irish

headmaster laid it down to me. After thirty minutes of wasting my life, He decided to suspend me permanently. He could have said that straight from the get-go. What I should have done, was expose my mum for being a drunk that didn't feed me, explain how I lived in a crime-riddled-estate, tell them to go fuck themselves before finally walking out. What I actually did, was sit with my arms crossed feeling sorry for myself. Disappointment followed, even though I was a perfect candidate for being a train wreck. That school was my only food source and the only place where I could block out my drunk mother, a life of crime, and chronic poverty. The only people I let down were my grandparents, and god forbid, there was no way I'd ever disrespect them. I wasn't even bad at that school. Some kids were awful. Soon after I left, I heard it went downhill. They needed to take a long hard look at the teachers, instead of their moral high ground. My morning tutor was an alcoholic that raged at us, the history teacher would drop his pencil to look up girls skirts, the woodwork teacher assaulted me, and the rest of the teachers were verbally abusive beyond discipline; not to mention the PE teacher having a relationship with a pupil. Still, nothing could change the fact that I was riding a wave to hell. What can young people say or do to be treated equally? By the time some of us were teenagers, we knew more about life than half of the adults. It was scandalous.

The only thing I missed about that school was the food and my English teacher who played with me on the corridor during breaks. Hiding behind doors, we pretended we were soldiers shooting at each other, throwing imaginary grenades. He brought his guitar into school to play in front of the class. One day he made a song up about me, playing it to the whole school in every lesson he had, making me famous. He knew I was going through a tough time at home. It went a little like this.

"Josephhhhhhhhh, Joseph Kane.

Josephhhhhhhhh, Joseph Kane.

I say a poor old Joseph,

a poor old Joseph,

poor old Joseph Kaneeee."

Everyone told me he sang that tune with his guitar for years after I left. Sadly, he ended up dying from cancer years later from smoking I imagined. He was a legend from Blackburn. I will never forget him. Fifty is too young for a good person to die. Scum bags live forever. The man dedicated his life to pupils like me. Now it's my turn to honour him, by doing the best I can in life for acknowledging me as a person, when others ignored me. Its people like him and my gran I want to make proud. It was worth getting kicked out. I had the best time of my life. If I listen carefully, I can still hear remnants of music played by Enya, from one of my classes. The only thing I possessed, was a porcelain flower I made for mum,

painted yellow for mothers day. The science department kept my rattlesnake skin that my relative brought from California. I let them keep it to show future pupils. What won't be missed, are the lonely walks through a dangerous park, when I woke up late. I doubt mum would notice if someone kidnapped me. I could be in France before she gained consciousness.

Just before being exiled from school, mum and I moved into a new flat with Levi. We stayed on the estate; it was just close to my dads old flat by the pubs. Now basking in the sun in Bournemouth, there was no worry of bumping into him again. I only saw him twice a year, and that was only because he visited my gran. He was another parent that had a selfish, strange, ignorance about him. Even still, I loved my dad, and he always said he loved me too; over the telephone of course. He told me I could go and live with him, but it never materialised. He just left me to the mercy of my mother. I had two parents that didn't want me; how charming. If they couldn't take care of me, what the hell am I doing on this planet? It took earth 4.543 billion years for two drunks to get together, only to decide they don't want me. The new flat was a shithole. We went from a perfectly good Council flat, started from scratch, just to move into a damp, private rented flat that was two streets away. I had no idea what went on in her head. It had to be because it was closer to a pub, that's the only logical explanation. Every time I came

back from school, no one was home. She was at the end of the street in the pub getting slaughtered. There was one time when she answered the door when I finished school, telling me about her great news.

"Oright mum! How's your day been mum! How are you mum!" She sarcastically said to me.

"You don't even ask how your mum is."

"By the way, I've just got married."

Give me a chance to get through the front door, Jesus! From out the blue, mum and her family went to the registry office, got married and then had a private meal together while I was at school. I didn't mind of course, Levi was a nice guy. I was the one that got them together, but she could have asked me if it's ok. It was strange having Levi's grandchildren, older than me, call me uncle Joseph. They took it serious as well. Even some of Levi's sons and his daughter introduced me as their brother. She didn't think twice about filling the freezer before eating a three-course meal, smiling for the camera with a glass of champagne in her hand. I knew why she married him. It was to get her hands on his money. She set up a joint bank account. Now his wife, she had a firm grip on him. Somehow their relationship worked. She never made it easy for him though.

Now at home all the time, the only thing to do is play Grand Theft Auto on my PlayStation 1. Without knowing, my generation was brainwashed by video games that depicted

crime. Our surroundings were nothing but a bad influence. The music artist 2pac was in full flow with his music career, and Hollywood released plenty of gangster movies. Adding those elements to our childhood development with the screwed up life we had, contributed to most of the crime we did. With so much bad influence, our minds were totally warped. There were only two outcomes in the future for most of us; prison or death. That seems like what someone in the Mafia would say; the only difference is, they had a choice to join that life, we didn't. Unlike organised crime, we did what we had to to survive. Everything was imposed on us from bad parenting. When a kid is brought up in a life of poverty, crime, and substance abuse, the last thing they need is a movie, a song, or a video game to encourage them. I could feel a tug of war in my mind between good and evil. With a short supply of positive role models, I think it's safe to say that future generations are fucked! With bad outweighing the good, I was sucked in by the vortex of instant gratification all around me. The buzz was too addictive.

Some guy with a black leather jacket walked to the shops from his high rise flat. He had a gym bag on his back that was chained around him. Apparently, it was full of beer from the shop, so we decided to rob him. Like a pack of wolves, we attacked him as he walked away ignoring us. Each of us tried to pull his bag off him. Surrounded, we tried everything to stop the grown man reaching his home. I kicked and

punched him with everyone else before jumping on his back like a Lion. Placing him in a chokehold, I tried to get my prey to the floor. Everyone ran out of ideas. I looked for a weakness, something I had been taught all my life. His legs were the only thing keeping him up, so I waited until he put his weight on his left leg. I kicked as hard as I could behind his knee so that he would fall from his own weight. He dropped like a sack of potatoes. The rest of the gang spectated, after failed attempts to stop him in the past.

"No way, Kane has got him."

Once on the floor, they ripped him to pieces like animals. By then, I walked away to the lads watching it. I couldn't kick someone when they were down. They beat him, robbed him, then left him to struggle home. He was a big tough guy. We were just a bunch of kids, but I felt terrible afterwards. How could everyone else find it so easy to be bad, when I found it so hard?

I went on to steal cars, got arrested one time, then witnessed a copper kick the shit out of my friend Lee for being cheeky. I moved on to slightly bigger things like shoplifting and smoking weed. No one ever told me what to do, or that it was wrong. Being out of school meant I had to go to a day centre. It was a place for naughty kids that received some form of education. Being on the estate, we adopted a new kind of language called backslang. I don't know where it came from, but the police couldn't understand a word we were saying to

each other. They eventually figured it out. I imagine it's now taught during police training because unless you know a simple concept, you wouldn't understand it. That was an amusing time while it lasted. Here are some examples.

Ya-goo = you

Way-got = what

Cay-gan = can

Ka-gum-agover-hay-gear = Come over here

Play-geese = Police

Ray-gun = run

Cay-gan-yagoo-gago-tagoo-theyga-shaygop = Can you go to the shop

Alternatively,

Keban-yeboo-gabo-taboo-thaba-sheb-op = Can you go to the shop

We ran rings around the police, destroyed the community along with our own life, even if we didn't realise. Whenever we wanted to call out to each other, we made a similar noise to what a dolphin makes. Our gang name was the first of its kind, later being copied in different variations for other gangs around Preston. The harder you look into an abyss, the deeper it gets. My intuition and wisdom pulled me back. I had reached as far as I could morally go. My dream was to join the Army or move to America. From the age of eight,

after watching action movies all my childhood, I wanted to be a proud soldier that fought and died for my country. The pinnacle of my existence with all my strength was to die on the battlefield with pride, to return to the void where I came from before my drunk parents met. There was no honour in crime or cowardly acts. Everyone is responsible for their own actions. We can't blame and follow footsteps, just because those before us, betrayed those before them. The life we had can't be stopped; it has to be syphoned off in a positive new direction. Each bad influence needs to be suffocated like a fire that's starved of oxygen. Energy in a being will always find an outlet. Direct that energy to something good and a new cycle will follow. Maybe I was crazy for seeking good, and life was inhospitable. All I know is, there is no way I'm spending ten years in prison, or dying at the age of forty from suicide, presuming drink, drugs or a knife doesn't kill me.

Living close to a Mosque, droves of kids in white religious clothing had to walk through our neighbourhood to get there. As well as pelting stones at them, two brothers equivalent to the Kray twins decided to attack them up in person. The kids were much younger, but they didn't care. Stealing piles of trainers from the mosque doorway weren't enough; they had to go one step further. As I was the only person with them at that time, what I witnessed shocked even me. The brothers grabbed as many kids as they could to attack them. They punched and kicked the ones that ran

past. The ones that didn't run were lynched. Having them in headlocks, they chocked the life out of them. The poor boys didn't say a word throughout the terrifying ordeal. I didn't know what to do. It was the last thing I expected. They bent the kids over their back, nearly snapping their spines. The squeals that echoed down the street made my skin crawl. For five minutes, they caused absolute carnage outside the Mosque. I never knocked about with them after that. It was nothing more than pure evil. When I think I've seen it all, something even more horrific happens. Some of the community got severely victimised over the years. The worst event had to be an elderly couple the same age as my grandparents. Their flat was located down a ginnel next to other flats in a really weird spot. Because most of the kids from that estate ran past, they habitually kicked the elderly couple's door. The couple would come out shouting, which only fuelled everyone to do it more. They asked the Council for a swap, but they didn't seem to care. They were victimised so bad over the years, they became ill and died. They had other health problems, but I believe they were tortured to death in their own home from the systematic trauma. There was no mercy on anyone that got targeted. It was an evil cartoon stuck on repeat.

"Mirror, mirror, on the wall.

Who's the worst one, of them all."

Being at home with mum was absolute hell on earth from the age of twelve onwards. It was cheaper to drink at home, so that's what she did. Now she had the bank of Levi, she was smashed every day. Kestrel super strength lager, with orange juice, was her poison. It stunk! How she could drink that shite, I'll never know. If I went out, I'd be coerced into some awful crime. If I stayed in, I had one hell of a night. I stayed in my room most of the time. The food situation hadn't improved; the cupboards were still empty. Her routine was to drink in her room talking crap all night to Levi with loud music. I honestly thought he would make her calm down. After getting her ass kicked by his daughter, her antics were magnified. Phil Collins, Police, and Sting vibrated through my wall as I tried to sleep. For no reason at all, fired up on loopy juice, she would come crashing through my door.

"Get the fuck up, and get in my room now. You have five seconds!"

I couldn't go back to sleep, because she would do the same thing until I complied. The hallway light shined around her head. All I could see was a thin shadow, with green eyes bulging out like a monster. After punching my door three or four times, she walked off waiting for me.

"Right, what the fucks going on? What the hell do you think you are doing?"

It was all a figment of her imagination. She didn't even know my favourite colour, let alone what I got up to. I just wanted to go to sleep. Now mentally unstable, she enjoyed

tormenting me for hours on end, depriving me of sleep. All Levi did was sit in silence, looking at the floor. Neither of us did anything wrong. She created it in her head like she wanted to fight someone, from the rocket fuel she drank. After hours of suffering, there was no sign of slowing down. Climbing back in bed made it worse.

"Will you fucking leave me alone."

Swearing at her gave her all the ammunition she needed. It made her worse as the night went on. Six hours later, she burnt herself out, falling asleep on the floor next to her music CDs. After an hour of sleep, the dragon awoke, doing precisely the same thing.

"Get in here now, you're taking the fucking piss out of me."

It didn't matter if I had school or not. Half of my detentions were from falling asleep in class. She ran a campaign of torment for years. Sat in my room one night watching a movie on the small television my grandparents bought, a sex scene came on. Hearing her coming towards my room, I tried to turn it off quickly. It was another excuse to start on me. She walked in before I could turn it off.

"What the fucking hell? You better get the fuck in here now. I can't believe this shit. Levi, he's watching fuckin porn. He's a dirty bastard; I want him out of my house."

She caused havoc for hours on end. Explaining it was an action movie called Timecop, with Jean-Claude Van Damme

didn't matter. It was all the excuse she needed. She was crazier than a shithouse rat.

The best part was when my mum's friends and family phoned up or came around. It was like flicking a switch on her back; talk about Jekyll and Hyde. She would go from a violent, aggressive, abusive person to Mary Poppins in two seconds flat. The snake with two heads revealed itself. She reminded me of Medusa. The torment was compared to sitting under a dripping tap, while water drops bounced off my head. Evil thoughts passed through my mind, while incredible anger overcame me, now that I was in full flow of puberty. All that I endured in my life was finally at the surface. I wanted to kill her. Everything my dad did to her had somehow become justified. We had two cats to help kill the mice in the back yard. It had the opposite effect. The cats would catch the mice, then bring them in as a gift. We originally had one cat, but it ran away. I would have done the same given the situation. Under the sink, we had some rat poison. As well as being terrified of spiders, my mum hated mice or creepy crawlies. Personally, I think she hated anything that lived. I placed some of the rat poison on the counter, before crushing it up with a lighter. I was so angry, I just wanted her to die. I mixed it with a cup of tea that I had made for her. It was probably enough to kill a small elephant. Looking down at the cup, her next hour was about to be her last. Consequences of the aftermath invaded my

thoughts. There was no reason to prolong my suffering or hers. There was no future other than a life of drink for this stranger called mum. Lying in her pit, I walked down the hall past my bedroom. Eventually, I was outside her room with a cup of tea that was about to change my life forever. Stood frozen, I became overwhelmed with doubt, guilt and every other emotion a good son would feel. Then I questioned myself. She doesn't know how lucky she is to have a caring, thoughtful son with a conscience. I threw the cup of tea down the sink. She wasn't worth it. Life will catch her up. It catches everybody up. I didn't know how much more I could take.

Fed up with how the flat looked, we moved house again for the umpteenth time. I suspected that we needed to run from debt collectors, but who knew what motivated mum. It was off the estate which was good, but not by much. The new neighbourhood was practically attached to my estate, close to my old high school. The faces didn't change; I just happened to live near different gang members. Chris bounced from flat to flat on the estate, being drawn into bad influences as much as me. He mainly played his music, having parties all the time, rather than hanging around the streets as I did. His generation was bad, but not as intense. Some bad black guy we knew stabbed him in the face, before robbing his music equipment right in front of him, out of his own home. As well as my challenges, he had his too. Things like that happened from time to time. Now in a two-bedroom house instead of a

flat, we had more room to relax in; another freezing shithole. We never had any heating in all the places we lived in. Mum had a heater in her bedroom, which took the piss. Her life resided in her bedroom. The last thing we needed was a bigger place. No one ever used the two living rooms. The area we moved to was a Muslim community, so it was good being in a calm environment. Their gang was always on the corner, but they were harmless, apart from the prick that punched me in school. Directly across from us, was a family that lived in two houses, side by side. There was an old Asian man in the house on the left, being looked after by his daughter. The house on the right belonged to his other daughter, that had quite a few kids. The two daughters were Chris's age, and they became good friends with Levi and my mum. They weren't devoted to Islam like most of the community. The old man was an alcoholic that had four daughters to a white woman. That didn't go down well being a Muslim. Siobhan that lived in the house on the left was a nice woman. Sharron with all the kids was also lovely, but just like my mum, she was a full blown alcoholic, very loud and very animated. With over five kids, she mainly stayed at home. Mum would drink with her across the road expectedly. I went across plenty of times. We became close to them. With the pigsty of a house, piles of clothes everywhere, and kids running around in nappies, Sharron usually stood in front of the fireplace, with a baby in one arm, and a glass of neat vodka in the other. During the chaos, she shouted at kids trying to act organised; it was a complete zoo. With the

whole family drinking, and taking substances, it was no wonder the rest of the community felt their impact. Everyone was intertwined or knew each other so the actions from one family could be felt across the estate. Bad influence plagued everyone, giving an incentive that its ok to do what the hell they want, because everyone is doing the same. Eight-year-olds smoked drugs and stole cars because everyone around was that way inclined. Once everyone had caught the scum-disease, it then evolves into a competition. Stories of places like Manchester and London echoed around, creating a standard that everyone lived up to. It became nothing short of crazy.

Being fourteen was one of the toughest years of my life. Dossing around all day had become the norm, along with most people in my situation. There were no plans whatsoever for my future. Now my only meal from school was no longer available; I somehow survived off toast. Mum received child benefit for me; I just didn't get any of it. Even Levi had disability benefits, yet the fridge had been empty wasting electric for years. It was only when her mum came around as a guest that she made an effort to cook a meal. It was the only time the living room was ever used. Suffering from mental health issues, my gran lived in a psychiatric ward for quite some time. Levi had a nightmare trying to get her back, come night time. As he drove down the road, she would open the car door trying to jump out. She didn't want to live

anymore. Poor Levi had to drive while holding her. It happened every week until he refused. Even when she visited, the only food I received was leftovers. Her excuse for starving me for years was because I didn't like her cooking. What kid isn't fussy about what they eat? Begging people I knew, I could make up forty pence to get something to eat. The takeaway up the road sold one japati for exactly forty pence. Pouring chilli sauce on warmed me up. That was my only source of food. Sometimes I walked to Fulwood to get a meal during the week from my gran. Having pride made me reluctant to ask anyone for anything. My mum didn't deserve me, the money she got, or Levi for that matter. One day when she was out of her room, I decided to search around for money. The first place I looked was under the mattress. Long behold, there was a shitload of money piled up in twenty-pound notes. It must have been payday. I hated stealing, but that was a day when I took what was rightfully mine. Forty pounds was all I took. The first thing I bought was cannabis. Getting through depression, and those nights of hell was a priority. Secondly, I bought some food from the takeaway, because I couldn't cook. By now, all the boys were selling weed and crack cocaine. They didn't let life drill them to the ground. Instead, they took the bull by the horns and survived. Now fairly distant away from that kind of life, I grinded it out living with mum.

Lying in bed on most nights, the same routine would occur. My bedroom door would be kicked open, then punched numerous times.

"Get the fuck up now. What have you said to Levi?"

She was good at making stories up. I tried reasoning with her, begging her to leave me alone. Insisting like usual, all I could do was respond.

"Just fucking leave me alone."

Her shouting drove me to despair, and now it was worse.

"Right that's it; I'm ringing the police."

She started taking it to the next level with threats. If it weren't the police, she would start ringing Levi's family up.

"Will you come and sort him out? I can't take it anymore." In a soft-spoken voice, dramatically playing the victim.

Her mind was puddled. I was threatened with violence from forty-year-old black men in my kitchen thanks to her; at fourteen. Her nights of drinking would go from music in the living room, dancing and laughing like an idiot, to psycho.

"Angie, will you leave him alone."

Levi tried until I told her to fuck off, then they were both against me. He raved on about getting one mother in life. I wish someone would take this mother and replace her.

"Right, that's it. I've had enough; get the fuck out."

"What do you mean get out?"

"I want you out now, or I'm ringing the police."

"Where am I supposed to go?"

"I don't care; I want you out. Nobody talks to me like that."

"Where am I supposed to go at 3am?"

"You should've thought about that before telling me to fuck off."

"Are you taking the piss, where am I supposed to fucking go?"

"Kiss my ass, then lick it!"

She always did have a way with words. It was at the point that being outside was a better alternative. Mentally, I couldn't take it anymore. I grabbed my thin jacket and stormed out. The streets were peacefully quiet. The weather was two degrees. There was no shelter or help I could seek. No ideas came to mind on how to survive the streets at such a late hour. The only shelter I could think of was in a police cell. Close the town was a car showroom. I looked for a brick to smash the window just to get arrested. Just my luck, I couldn't find one. There was a three-storey block of flats close by, so I headed there. The stairs were exposed to outside elements, only providing half the shelter. My body temperature dropped if I sat in one spot for more than ten minutes, so I moved around or went for a walk. With nothing but my jumper and I thin jacket, I pulled my arms inside my sleeves to stay warm in a squat. In four or five hours I'll head back. Maybe by then, she will be asleep. When I knocked, the

outcome was 50/50. If she answered the door, I was screwed.

"What do you want? You're not coming in."

When Levi answered, he would stand quietly as I walked upstairs to my bed. Knowing she didn't sleep long before the whole thing kicked off again, I sometimes got an hour sleep. I even hid in the house, listening to what she talked about. She usually caught me after a sweep of the house.

"Joseph? Has he gone out? I don't fucking believe this. Levi, when I was young, If I ever spoke to my mum and dad like that, I'd get a smack across my head. Joseph doesn't know how lucky he is."

"Lucky?.... Lucky?.... Is she having a fucking laugh." I mumbled to myself around the back of the sofa.

Once distracted, she went back to her bullshit stories about how her dad listened to 'My Way' by Frank Sinatra, topping up her glass of loopy juice on her bedside table, with a lamp that had a manky yellow bulb. Levi just sat up in bed staring at the wall, being took in by her every word. Her new trend was to kick me out nearly every night at 3am. She knew I had nowhere to go at that time in the morning. Preparing to face the cold, I stole a bottle of brandy that she had in one of the cupboards. I saved a can of coke to go with it. The next time she kicked me out, I took the drinks with me. Being prepared was important that night, with the temperature well below freezing and snowing. With no winter clothes, the only way I

could stay warm was to drink some brandy and coke. Alcohol was disgusting, but it went down a treat with coke. Internally it warmed me up nicely. Sitting on that cold slab of concrete at the top of the exposed stairs, a million thoughts and memories went through my head. What will be of my future in its current state? How the hell did everything get so bad? Whenever I needed the bathroom, I found a bush with some large leaves used for toilet paper. It was so cold during the night. Moving around so much wasted energy that I couldn't spare. Already thin, if I stopped moving for more than ten minutes, I'd shiver uncontrollably. After walking for miles on end, I had discovered there was a waiting room at Preston train station. The room had heaters blowing some really good warmth. The heat made me tired, so I laid down and accidentally fell asleep. Sleeping right through to morning, when I woke up, the room had filled with people in suits reading newspapers, and drinking coffee. I felt like such a tramp, as I pulled my arms from out of my jacket. The security man told me that people are not allowed to sleep, so I never returned. The heat was guaranteed to knock me out if I went back. I was ashamed of how I looked and dressed. Somewhere along my life, I became very self-conscience and shy. I'd rather starve to death, or squat over a bed of nails than do anything that people frowned upon. With my gang, I felt like I belonged somewhere. I felt like the most confident person in the world, able to do anything without repercussions.

Nothing I could say or do could make my mum change the way she was. Now eclipsed, she was out of reach from everyone. During the day she went backwards and forwards across the road, sometimes making a scene in front of Siobhan and Sharron. She always started in the most subtle way, while portraying herself as a good person, so that no one knew what she was like behind closed doors. I became good friends with Siobhan. Her fiancé had left her for someone else, leaving her devastated; what a big mistake he made. Siobhan was beautiful, intelligent, and funny. At the time, she had a few glasses of vodka each day to try and get over it, but never got drunk. I opened up to her about what my mum was putting me through. She took me under her wing offering me food and a place to lay low in her dad's house. My mum started noticing that I had found a safe haven, so she upped her antics. One day she decided to call the police when I went for a walk up Beacon Fell with my uncle.

"My son has gone to commit suicide; can you send someone."

Mick and I didn't know. Two police horses walked right past us near the top of the hill, popular for fell walkers. Once back in Preston, we were approached by the police. She had completely lost the plot. I couldn't understand why my mum had it in for me so much. She seemed to enjoy it. Cannabis wasn't strong enough to help me deal with the daily torment, so I started self-harming. Inside I was screaming, but she

146

didn't know. Taking a large bread knife out of the kitchen, I sliced across the top of my arm. The jagged edge created wide cuts every time I sliced without looking. The pain from my arms took my mind off her torture, hidden under my jumper. Anger was an understatement. Why on earth did I not use the rat poison? I could have been out of prison by the time I reached twenty, with a trade. Not satisfied with what she had already done, she rung the police, telling them I had a gun. Luckily, when armed police had come looking for me, I was sat in Siobhan's house. Mum knew we were inside together, so she told the police where I was. They banged on her door so hard; I thought they would break it down. My heart pounded as they surrounded the house. It was terrifying. Siobhan calmed me down, instructing me to creep into the kitchen with her until they left. I could hear my mum talking like butter wouldn't melt in her mouth. Thank heavens they went. Over the next few days, I had to hide while armed police hunted me down. I loved to take the chase from the police innocently, but this was different. The result would have been me on the floor with guns in my face, or worse, they might have shot me. Armed police followed my Uncle Mick for days, in the hope he would lead them to me. It ended when I surrendered to the police station. They locked me up for ten hours before releasing me. What kind of mother wants her son to suffer, or be killed?

Anger filled my veins when I finally exploded in a rage of fury. She was trying to kick me out one day, which was unusual. She usually waited until the early hours of the morning. Something inside me just snapped. In my face shouting with her stinking breath stood on the landing, I pushed her flying into her bedroom door. Being that she was as thin as me, she crashed to the floor like a small child. The look on her face was priceless; she looked like she had seen a ghost.

"I'm sick of your fucking shit, YOU get the fuck out and see how you like it."

Like a possessed demon, the cannabis must have clouded my judgment. She scurried downstairs out of the house, like the coward she was with her tail between her legs. Walking right behind her, I slammed the interior door smashing the glass window when it hit the wall. She fell to the floor in the middle of the road looking back at me with fear. I picked up a shard of glass from the floor, aiming straight for her like Michael Myers. She begged for her life in the middle of the road as I got closer, with the full intention to scare the shit out of her. I had learnt that fear was a powerful tool. As I looked to my right, the Muslim gang stood on the corner staring at me, so I returned inside. I dropped the glass, waiting for an ambulance to arrive. Her collarbone had snapped in half when I pushed her into the door. Amazingly, she didn't get me arrested. I did, however, get permanently kicked out.

There was only one person I could turn to, and that was Chris. Now off the estate, he had a flat down by the river. Fortunate to let me stay, Chris told me how mum had kicked him out as a teenager, making him sleep in a bin when it was snowing. I slept on a mattress for a few months behind his sofa. He stayed up playing on his PlayStation with his girlfriend. We both had the same idea to distance ourselves from that hell hole of a neighbourhood. It was only a matter of time before we would have been sucked in. What followed was nothing more than pure destruction.

1. Countless suicides.

2. Countless deaths from drink/substance abuse.

3. Carjackings.

4. Shootings/drive-by shootings

5. Prostitution.

6. Armed Robbery.

7. Gang wars.

8. Murders.

9. Burglary.

10. Intimidation/violence

11. International drug and gun smuggling.

The list goes on. Everything you can think of, they did it. From the small kids I watched grow, to the older men;

everyone was involved in serious crime amounting to 300-400 years in prison between the lot of them over two decades and counting. Finally, the estate was knocked down. Dead, in prison, or misplaced, it all came to an end as I predicted. A drug ring was smashed that was described as Lancashire's largest-ever police operation. The black guy that stabbed Chris in the face was smuggling drugs and guns from Holland. Being brought down, he took a lot of people with him to prison, including my friend that told the teacher to fuck off on my first day at primary school. It spread like wildfire. I couldn't believe the people I grew up with went to such lengths. Brothers and sisters all shared the same fate. Sure, they had nice kitchens, nice cars, and made the national news along with an hour-long documentary, but it didn't justify the shit life we had. That's why I stopped running. In the end, it all catches up. Another portion of the gang had also made headline news when a serious crime unit was sent from London to surveillance them. A Few years younger than me, the group were caught selling drugs around Preston before the gang was smashed. Some of the faces were new, but either way, anyone involved had to chew the same fat. They proved the point that they were bad mother fuckers. In the end, they gained nothing.

A few years in prison will only make them sharpen their tools. They come out worse than when they went in. In my experience, it takes fifteen years to get over something that's

had a profound effect. Career criminals don't need locking up; they need separating from society for fifteen years, to change. There should be somewhere secure for such a long time, not because of a crime, but because it takes so long to change their mindset. Imagine a white shirt being placed in a washing machine with twenty pink shirts. That white shirt will turn pink. Only after countless washes later, will that shirt become a sort of white again. Politicians and the justice system are narrow-minded and ignorant. Criminally minded people can adapt. Prison is a dating factory for like-minded people to get together. What criminals can't adapt to, is the loss of habit, loss of memory, and change. Time, not punishment is the only way to change a person. Give them access to equipment and resources to fulfil their ambitions or hobbies, and they could be rehabilitated in ten years. As long as they show a strong desire for what they love, and granted the government provides those resources, no matter how expensive or extreme it may be, they will be reformed. Right or wrong, good or evil, the energy within people needs an outlet. Criminals communicating with one another in prison still represents pink shirts mixed together. They should only interact with noncriminals for a long time before change can happen. I could be wrong. Maybe they need locking up forever.

My good friend Siobhan drank herself to death years later. I had failed to be there for her like she once was for me. One of

her sisters died from substance abuse, so she hit rock bottom. Sharron finally lost her kids to social services but was the surviving sibling out of four sisters. The fourth sister committed suicide years prior. One of Levi's sons ended up getting life in prison for kidnap and chopping off someone's finger over drug money. Derek died from alcoholism. Unfortunately, Rocky had to be put down because he tried to attack everyone once Derek passed away. My dad's friend Bluey also died from alcoholism, along with Stan-the-man who stood outside the pub laughing and joking.

Armageddon had arrived. Everyone dropped like flies. It was easy come, easy go. So much for being a pussy; bunch of idiots. I had more brains in my little finger compared to any of them. I had a gift that no one possessed; common sense. Their lifestyle was not sustainable, and I knew it from day one. It was only a matter of time before they faced reality. Surprisingly, it all happened within a short space of time. I thank god for looking over me. I had walked the ultimate tight rope for years. Anxiety took over me whenever I got close to the estate. It took a long time before I could return. Now its all gone in the blink of an eye. Instead of embracing that life like 99.9% of people, I sat back and did the opposite. It was like watching a flower grow from nothing, only to wither and die. I watched kids innocently run around without a care in the world, before being shaped and groomed into a criminal ideology. Now I feel nothing but

sadness over the rise and fall, over what could have been good folk in different circumstances. It makes me wonder what these people could have achieved. They were certainly able, and way beyond my capabilities. No one is born bad. I prayed for God to have different plans for me; after all, I was only a teenager.

Chapter 6 - Bad News

Now away from my dreaded mum, it was good to relax with Chris and his friends enjoying some good laughs. They drank sociably, and I smoked the odd bit of weed. Hating tobacco and alcohol, my usual thing was to smoke cannabis from a bong made from a can of coke. With my mum spending all my child benefit, I never had a penny, so smoking weed was very rare. The stress was gone, leaving me with no need to smoke it. It felt great being a normal teenager, being able to eat food every day. My Uncle Mick continued to pick me up at weekends so we could go and watch Preston North End. My dad started to visit my gran now his life was back on track. Now sober, he drove up on his new superbike. He was an adrenaline junkie. Having put some weight on, he looked great with his new tan. At least someone was happy. He had no idea what shit I was going through. Not paying much attention to me, Mick and I continued having fun like two kids. The only person my dad loved was my gran, along with tons of other people that loved her. She didn't judge or put anyone down, but instead, selflessly did her best to help people for no good reason. Now that my Uncle Kevin, who I wasn't close to, had a child on the way, I was no longer going to be the only grandchild. During the summer, we all travelled down to stay at my dads flat in sunny Bournemouth. With my grandad's careful driving, it took six hours to get down in a car with five people, no leg room and suitcases pushing against our headrest. Whenever we passed

a pub when Mick was driving, my grandad would let us know.

"Pull in!"

My gran kept him on a very short leash. On arriving in Dorset, it was a beautiful place to see. The nature reserve we passed looked natural. So natural in fact, that we ended up running over a peacock that smashed the windscreen. My grandad had to punch the windshield out with his fist so he could see where he was driving at sixty miles per hour. On arrival in one piece, and everyone with cramp, my dad met us at his front door. He rented an upstairs flat with two bedrooms in a pleasant area. It was very smart inside. He had leather settee's and a real tiger skin on his wall that his uncle shot in Africa during the war. That night we relaxed in front of the television, with plates of Chinese food on each lap. We had a great week going to restaurants, the beach, watched a football match, then later we all drove to Poole. My grandparents loved visiting coastlines. We looked in shops, ate fish & chips and watched the boats go out. Nothing beats a ray of sunshine with a jar of cockles saturated in vinegar. Parched peas that my gran loved, on the other hand, made me want to vomit. She poured enough salt on to kill a colony of slugs. Mick loved eating oysters, somehow coercing me to try them. Without choking, I honestly don't know how I swallowed it in one. We created some great family albums from the trips we took. I wish I could have shown my friends from the estate that life could

be good and that it didn't have to be bad. The further away from Preston I reached, the happier I was. Sadly, I had to return.

"Oh my god, it's finally happened. The news I have been waiting for my entire life. I'm so happy. Everyone is going to be so jealous when they find out."

"You better go and ask your mum."

"What? She's not going to stop me. I won't let her."

"Your dad is coming anyway, so she can't really stop you."

....

"Mum, my grandma has booked a three-week holiday to Florida, so can I go?"

"No, you're not going."

"Yes, I am."

"No you're not, and that's that."

"You can't stop me; I'm old enough."

"You're not sixteen yet haha."

"Well everyone wants me to go, and my dad's going so you can't stop me."

"Watch me."

Against all odds, by Phil Collins that she always played, she was fighting a losing battle. She knew she had been defeated

because my dad was on my birth certificate. Now wiser, I threatened her with social services and benefit fraud, knowing damn well her first priority was drinking. Little more than a whisper stopped her from preventing me. Her silence said it all when she walked off to her bedroom. It was a small victory as I advanced towards independence.

Shopping for summer clothes with my gran made the trip sink in, while I filled my suitcase with shorts, t-shirts, and snorkelling equipment. My grandparents, Mick, dad, my Uncle Kevin, his wife and two kids prepared for the taxi to take us to Manchester airport. Anticipation barely kept me still for more than two minutes. My window seat was something I had to hustle for. Taking off was amazing. I was fortunate enough to go to Sweden on a student exchange with my last primary school, but this was even better. We all smiled, as the plane took off heading towards the clouds. The view was amazing. The plane skimmed across the blanket of clouds, with a golden-brown sky from the unobscured sun that shined through my window. Happy endings happen after all. I stuck my middle finger up at Preston on the way to Scotland before darting across the Atlantic Ocean. On my cassette player, I had fitting music for that exact moment I had planned since childhood. "In your face mum!" The one thing that kept me from serious crime was the reality of being refused entry into the US. Everyone couldn't possibly

expect me to live in that shithole forever. I had a sunny beach to go to. Who cared, I was on my way to paradise.

Once we got there, a private minivan we hired for three weeks was waiting for us. My Uncle Kevin drove us to the Villa we had arranged. What a dream place. It looked exactly how I imagined it, but better. The cul-de-sac was something out of a movie like E.T. Our Villa had a swimming pool out in the back, next to a golf course, enclosed under a mosquito cage. The first day we had a barbecue by the pool, relaxing. By night time we looked like lobsters. Crickets in the grass called out all night confirming that it was Florida. Tragedy was never far behind where ever I went. My Uncle Kevin's two-year-old son had fallen into the swimming pool head first. No one was around. It happened so fast. Sinking to the bottom like a rock, the holiday was about to be over. Being at the other end of the pool, I froze while he reached the bottom. Quickly springing into action, I dived under to find him. His limp body was like pulling a suction cup off a glass table with the lack of gravity in the water. Being a skinny kid myself, I pulled him out of the pool. Apart from a mouth full of water, a cry reassured me that he would be just fine. What a nightmare that could have been. The first week, we didn't see my dad because he took a detour to New Orleans before we had arrived in America. Every day was filled with activities with so much to do. There was no way we could see it all in three weeks. Having the minivan on the front, by the

time we got inside to go out for the day, the heat inside was a hundred and twenty degrees before air conditioning kicked it. Each morning was like being in an oven. Going to all the theme parks was such a blast. The first park had to be Disney World. From morning to night, we didn't stop for two minutes. My gran went on her favourite ride, 'it's a small world.' Later I had my picture taken with Mickey, Minnie, and Tigger. If the smile on my face got any bigger, I think it would have stayed like that. Full up on three hotdogs and a gallon of Pepsi, we went on rides all day, watched the parade, and then finally the fireworks before they closed for the night. It was spectacular. The following few days we hit the rest of the theme parks. Universal Studios was something I had never imagined. The movie-themed rides blew me away. From the age of eight, I was obsessed with Terminator 2 watching it every day, so to find out they had a T2 ride experience, I was emphatic. Before visiting Animal Kingdom, the star of the show had to be the Incredible Hulk roller coaster. With everyone's legs hanging in thin air, the ride ascended slowly. Not knowing what to expect, it gave everyone a false sense of security. Seconds into the ride, it catapulted straight up blowing my shoes off almost, before turning upside down into a corkscrew when it reached the top. The queue took nearly an hour, but boy was it worth it three times in a row. It was more exhilarating than being chased by cops. We roamed around taking in as much as we could with never a dull moment.

My gran's brother lived in Florida, so we visited him and his family. I was so jealous he lived there. His twenty-one-year-old daughter Tina took us to a lake jet skiing for the day. She was gorgeous, what a babe and fearless too. She showed us how to do one hundred and eighty degree turns at high speed, throwing whatever two people were riding it clean off. I don't know why I was nervous; I'd been riding motorbikes since I was twelve without helmets, flying over ramps that threw me off. My dad took me on his Superbike at ninety miles per hour down Blackpool Road, so how hard could it be? Going last, Tina shouted me.

"Jump on Joseph."

"OK."

"Are there Crocodiles in this lake?"

"Yes, there is."

"Erm, where should I put my hands?"

She grabbed my hands, placing them around her waist.

"Hold on tight."

What a rush. Being a small teen, every time she did a turn at fifty miles per hour, I flew off the back still holding on to her concussed. We pierced the water like an arrow, going deep under from the projection. The weight of her from the force, mixed with the thought I was about to land on top of a crocodile, scared the shit out of me. For the second we stopped deep under, there was no other place I'd rather be. Time had stopped for what felt like an eternity. I had been

reborn after feeling baptised while submerged. Still holding on to beauty, I reflected on all my ugly experiences. All the pain and suffering had vanished for that one moment. My mum undoubtedly was at home drinking her life away, while my old friends were sabotaging theirs in a life they couldn't escape. Meantime, I was lying at the bottom of a lake in Florida. It was funny how life turned out. Like my cousin that nearly drowned, I fought hard to continue with life. I fought hard to resurface after my out-of-body experience.

Visiting half a dozen beaches that month, the day at Clearwater beach was particularly nice. Palm tree's swayed in the wind, creating a bristling noise. Barefooted, my feet burnt from the fine hot sand, before quickly sinking to cooler sand. Each step took me closer to where I wanted to go. Looking around, I witnessed nothing but peace or the love everyone had for their families. Children made sand castles, while their mum and dads sunbathed on chairs. People swam without fearing judgment or blame. In shorts and a t-shirt, I walked past a temporary space, before it was time to have fun. Reaching the shoreline, I looked out over the horizon. Preston was 4,288 miles across the water. I didn't want to return. The thought of going back was unbearable. My future had no forecast whatsoever. So much time had passed before reaching this one moment to live my dream. What if I stayed? What if I ran away, disappearing across America? The thoughts turned into a plan I was going to

execute. If I keep my head down, I could easily find food and shelter somewhere. My plan was crushed by the thought of worrying my family or upsetting my gran after everything she had done for me. I knew it would be years before returning. Still, I was forever grateful for the best three weeks of my life. The experience had shaped me, but keeping that shape was anyone's guess. After cleaning the Villa, we had one last look to make sure we didn't forget anything. I was the last person to leave the house, taking in the feeling one last time. Looking through the blinds in one of the bedrooms, everyone put their suitcases in the back of the minivan. Something prompted me to lift the mattress my dad had slept in. I was in complete shock at what I was looking at. Without telling anyone, I carried with me dads little secret.

After returning home, it felt as if misery, worry, and stress were waiting at the airport. Living with Chris wasn't going very well. His small flat made everything awkward. Being around him, was the most time I had ever spent with him. Having different dads, he taunted me for everything my dad had done. We didn't have much in common apart from the life we had. There was something about him that seemed off. He walked around with a big chip on his shoulder. If there were no sugar or salt in the house, he would skitz out at his girlfriend. He had a controlling kind of ego like mum did. More often I went to my grandparent's house on the bus.

Now older, no one had to look after me. I surprised my gran every time I visited her at work. At the back of the hospital, she sorted the laundry out on a mammoth scale. Her colleagues were nice to me. One week, the conversation came up about moving me in with the three of them. I jumped for joy over the idea. Personally, it should have happened years ago. No one knew what my mum did because I kept it to myself. They knew she caused lots of trouble; they just didn't know how bad things had got. Chris didn't care less where I went, and neither did my mum. Coming close to fifteen, it was a done deal. Having my own room was a sanctuary. They didn't like me staying off school all day, so they got me into a local high school. It was my last year in school, with the reality of no qualifications, but I did it anyway. Things seemed to look up.

Arriving at the new school was nerve-racking. Being out of education for a year had changed me. Everyone knew each other for years, then a complete stranger like me arrives. Two of my childhood friends attended, Phil and Andy, but they were in the year below me. You could tell their parents took their time to build romance before conceiving. My parents would have got pissed, then jumped straight into bed, BISH BASH BOSH! All the kids looked at me from the whole school. I stood out like a saw thumb. Anxiety and worry followed me every single day. Out of coincidence, one of the Muslim boys from near my mums attended. He knew

my reputation, and who I was before telling the rest of the lads in my year. That day forward, I was watched over, protected and respected by the hardest lads in that school from different gangs around Preston. I don't why that happened, I didn't exactly have a claim to fame, but it was instant respect, especially from all the Muslim lads. Not everyone appreciated how I appeared from thin air, gaining more respect than they did, so it caused a bit of friction. It was mainly from one lad that couldn't take his eyes off me. I could see it in his eyes that he wanted to do me over. He had a black girlfriend that took a liking to me, which didn't help. Sexually active by then, I took his girlfriend off him. He was so pissed off. She was hot as well. We kissed in the alley after school near my grandparent's house, rubbing hands all over each other. My hands rubbed up her skirt grabbing her ass, while she tried to calm me down. The urge to touch and kiss girls drove me nuts at fifteen. Most of my time at that school, I shared a class with the cock of the school called Jamie. He was massive lad for his age that looked like Griff from Back to the Future 2. Not only was he big, but he was as hyperactive as me. With random actions, he would pick up chairs and launch them across the room at pupils entering the room. The chance that one of the legs would stick into someone's eyes was pretty high. Being under the wing of a dragon, it was no concern of mine. I had spent my entire life under the wing of numerous dragons. No one wanted to be on the receiving end. Having my own front door key, I was

able to nip home at dinner time to get some dinner. It felt great calling it my new home.

Everything went smooth for the first three months at school. Bonfire night had just passed when I decided to save a few fireworks for myself, from a few of the boxes that my family had stored in the spare bedroom. The idea was stupid, but I did it anyway. The next morning, I took some fireworks with me to school, setting off a few on the grass on the way there. It was only to show off. Later that day I had misbehaved, so one of the teachers sent me to sit in the library on my own, to think about my actions. Apart from the librarian, I was the only pupil in the room, just behind a wall that blocked our line of sight. Twiddling my thumbs, boredom had set in. Reaching for my bag, I played with the fireworks in my hand while pretending to read a book. Playing with the flint on the lighter, an idea came over me to put the flame close to the fuse. If it lights, then I'll put it out with my finger. If it doesn't light, then I'll put it away. The heat ignited the fuse. Panic came over me. Licking my fingers, I covered the fuse to put it out. With the fuse disappearing, it reappeared at the other end of my fingers, burning straight through. With seconds to go, it was about to explode in my face. A thought came over me to pull the fuse out, but I was worried that gunpowder might ignite it. Holding an air-banger in my hand with not much choice, it was either her or me, and it wasn't going to be me. I threw the fucker straight to the other

side of the room near the woman. Knowing World War III was about to start, I hid behind the wall covering my ears until the nightmare was over. The last thing that librarian expected that morning, was a firework to be thrown at her.

"eeerrrrrrrrrrrrrcccchhhhhh......"

"BANG!"

Unable to see or look from behind the wall, I quickly sat back in my seat with burnt fingers acting inconspicuous after hearing the lady dive to the floor. She ran towards the library doors looking like she had been dragged through a bush, before looking at me.

"Did someone just come in here?"

"I don't know."

We looked confused at each other. Within two seconds, she knew it was me.

"I'm going to get the headmaster; stay there!"

"Shit!"

I had done it this time. Not knowing what to do, I stored the rockets I had wrapped in bubble wrap under the bookshelf on the floor. No one would find them unless they had a good look. Next, I looked at the damage before running out of school quickly. The firework had burnt the carpet, then exploded against a wall. I was lucky. If that room had set on fire, my life would have been over. Ashamed, I went to my mums to stay for a few days. Telling her what happened was

the worst thing I ever did. The school and my grandparents knew it was me, and I couldn't return until I had a meeting with the headmaster. No one had to be a genius to figure out I was getting expelled. That night, my mum got drunk when the moon was full, before turning into something other than human, like she does every night. Strangely, she didn't kick my door in or wake me up. Instead, she called the fire brigade at 3am.

"Can you please send someone to my son's high school, he has hidden fireworks in children's books, so when they open them, they will explode in the child's face."

I couldn't believe it. What the hell was wrong in this woman's head? Why the hell would anyone say such a stupid thing? The fire brigade drove to my school, dragged the caretaker out of bed to unlock the doors, then searched for fireworks for three hours amongst ten thousand books. They found the rockets, but still had to check there were no traps. I made silly mistakes, but my mum's brain was warped from all the shite she drank, concealing my fate at that school. My grandparents were upset, forcing my dad to come from Bournemouth to attend the meeting with my mum. How inconvenient that must have been for him now I know his little secret. Being the first and last meeting they had attended in my entire school life, the headmaster gave a running commentary of what happened. They kicked me out, with no other way to fix it. In the car park, my mum and dad started bickering about each other's failures. I broke down

crying with my hands over my face. Not over what happened, but from the trauma I went through since birth. My mum went to cuddle me, so I pushed the sadistic bitch away. Then my dad went to hug me as he filled up with tears, while I wept on his black leather jacket. Returning to my Grandparents, I mainly stayed in my room before being hit with even more bad news in the following weeks.

During our holiday to Florida, my gran had found a lump on her breast. Keeping it quiet for a short time, she was sent to do some test at the hospital. What a major blow. Out of all the people in the world, why did she have a lump? Why not my mum or one of my criminal friends that didn't value life. With the test coming back as cancer, everyone was shell shocked. Intensive treatment started to try and eradicate it, beginning with the removal of her left breast. The thought of it made me quiver. She tried to show me the scar later on, but I couldn't look. Any sight of blood made me weak at the knees. She kept strong over the diagnoses, but she still had a long way to go. Further test revealed it was in her blood. The next stage was chemotherapy. It made her sick which is what we all wanted to avoid. The chemo was worse than the disease. This was the queen of the family that organised everything. If anything should happen, the rest of us would be in despair. She didn't represent a branch breaking off a tree; she was the tree. If she fell, we fell. The thought of losing her terrified the family. Mick and my grandad couldn't

even use a washing machine. Being just over sixty shortly after retirement, she wasn't even old. After weeks pulling her guts up in the toilet, hair fell all around the house. The wigs she had to wear looked stupid. There was no comparison to her real hair. Not realising the seriousness of the matter, the family tried their best to get on with things. Returning to the hospital for further test, it was more bad news. She had terminal cancer. It reached her bone marrow. My grandad promised to get a bone marrow transplant, but we all knew it wasn't realistic. It travelled through her precious body.

Being the strong stubborn woman my gran was, she continued to prepare for New Year's Eve, knowing it was her last. With all her energy, she put on the biggest party ever. Going into 2001, the moment had to be marked on a grand scale. We rented out a marquee tent for the side of the house with so many people expected. Live for today, and let tomorrow take care of itself she always said. Everyone had a good time on my gran's orders. We all had to put on a brave face, but we knew she was running out of time. All we could do was smother her with love as she did for so many.

Weeks after the party, my dad phoned up to speak to my gran. He was upset about something. Stood on the balcony upstairs, I earwigged nearly every conversation over the last few years. From that conversation, he seemed to be crying. She tried to get it out of him as to why he was crying.

"What is it love, tell me."

"I'm....I'm...I'm gay."

"Well it's alright, I still love you the same. Me and your dad love you no matter what you are."

Then I ran downstairs.

"See, I told you he was gay; my mum has been telling me since I was six."

"Get upstairs you!"

After going back to my room, she relayed the message to my dad.

"Joseph just said Angela has been telling him since he was six."

After getting off the phone, my grandad wanted to know what all the fuss was about.

"What's wrong with him now."

"He said he's gay."

"He's gayyyy."

My granddad couldn't believe it, which was surprising after all the fights he had with my dad. They never got along; in fact, they hated each other. Kevin was the hard-working number one son, as Mick always described him. My dad was a rebel. He wanted to get it off his chest before she died. My mum had been drilling it into my head for years.

"Your dads a fucking queer, a bisexual that sticks his dick into another man's ass."

She pushed her index finger up and down in the air motioning it.

"He only had you to prove he wasn't gay. I found a gay porn magazine under his bed."

It's great knowing my origins from the age of six, along with how the birds and bees worked. I always called my friend's gay; it was a popular insult. It never occurred to me when my dad went mad, every time I called Mick a faggot. Chris had been calling me a faggot for as long as I can remember, thanks to my dad beating mum up. At the same time my dad phoned up, he had just got back from Thailand. He didn't want to go, but my gran insisted. There was a rumour going around in my family that he had his drink spiked, was raped by four men and had his money stolen along with his passport. After everything I'd already seen, it didn't shock me. I felt bad for him, even though he abandoned me to live his gay life. It made no difference to me what he was. He was my dad, and I loved him. I couldn't say the same for my mum.

Approaching March, my gran had become very sick. Struggling to walk, she fell on the floor breaking her leg in the living room where we shared so many happy memories. Merciless cancer ate through her blood and bones like she

was nothing. I watched the paramedics take her away, knowing that was the last time she would ever see that house. Someone in the family phoned my dad, telling him to get on a train. When he arrived, he visited her during the morning, then vanished during the day raising my suspicions. Any other father would spend time with his son. He never even looked at me. I knew he was going to the pub, so I decided to search his bags. There was a bottle of vodka in one of the zips. It was clear he relapsed. Before leaving the Villa in Florida, I found an empty bottle of whiskey under his bed with a picture of a steamboat on the Mississippi River. Later that night, I confronted him about the vodka bottle. The cat was out of the bag. After confronting him, he didn't even make an effort to hide it, coming back every night drunk. His only concern in life was the bottle and his mum. He didn't help the situation or support any of us. I was so angry for never giving a toss about me.

Visiting the hospital my gran served for years with Mick and my grandad, we walked down an endless corridor into what felt like a new postcode. Even the grim reaper would get lost in that place. Arriving on her ward, they spoke to the doctor who informed us that she didn't have long left. My poor gran was so depressed, she rested on her right side staring at the wall without saying a word. She had every right to be pissed off. She was the one person on the planet that didn't deserve to suffer or die. The visit was cut short. Being men, I don't

think they could deal with it. They both said goodbye to her with a kiss, but she didn't flinch. I stopped myself from hugging or kissing her because I'd never seen her look so serious. She scared me. Those two had already walked away holding off the tears. I paused looking at her blank, emotionless face, before walking away with my head down. That image will stay with me forever. That night after more visits from her close family, she peacefully passed away. March 2001 marked the death of our queen. I will forever kick myself for not saying goodbye. I didn't know how to feel about death, or what it felt like to never see someone again. The whole experience felt strange. After her passing, my dad gave up on life getting drunk. Mick told him to go home until the funeral; he wasn't helping anyone but himself. The next day before returning home, he stood in the living room drunk with his black leather coat on, waiting for my uncle to take him to the train station. Stood alone in a room of silence, I looked hard at him. Nearly coming of age, it was about time I had a few words with him before departing. Positioning myself opposite the dinner table, I kept clear in case he became violent. That was the table I shared countless birthday parties and Sunday meals with my family. Quickly picturing in my head what I'd say if I were an adult, he was about to get both barrels of the shotgun. I knew damn well he wouldn't return for the funeral. Deep down, it was probably the last time he would ever be seen again. From his previous self-harming, overdoses, and near-death experiences from a failing liver, the odds were stacked.

"You're a bum, a loser that walked out on me, leaving me to suffer at the hands of my mum. She put me through hell because of you. You never loved me. You only cared about your selfish gay life down south. I'll be more of a man than you will ever be. Once I join the Army, I will show you what a real man is."

I gave him a right grilling. He just looked at the floor drunk, while his fifteen-year-old son told him off. I knew I had guts, determination, and courage to do anything with my life. I don't know what his problem was. His sexuality didn't bother me. It was beyond a joke how two selfish drunks could legally have a child, leaving my grandparents to pick up the pieces. After getting it off my chest, I went for a walk until they left. Stood in the ally I had been running up and down throughout my childhood, I watched them drive off.

With only days away from the funeral, the family made arrangements for the service. Resting in the caretakers, I decided to go with Mick and my grandad to see her for one last time. Not giving her a hug or a kiss in the hospital, it was only right that I quietly said my goodbyes. That was the first time I had seen a dead body. Stood by the wall, there was no way I could get any closer. I expected her to move, or worse sit up. The whole week felt like a bad dream. Without knowing the first thing about death, I said a few words in my head. They both kissed and said goodbye to her. She was wearing one of her white suits with that horrible wig she had

to wear. Rosary beads bonded her hands together, neatly on her stomach. There was one thing cancer couldn't take, and that was all the wonderful memories she created. No one would ever forget all the love she gave or the times she went out of her way to help someone. She will be etched in time forever. Guilt came over me from all the times I was naughty or made her cry. Influence from the estate rubbed off on me, creating a constant battle of good and bad. The two conflicted, each time I went backwards and forwards between the two environments. Being the lady she was, I'm sure she would forgive me if I ever had the chance to say sorry.

Arriving at the church she got married in at eighteen, a few people stood outside. Is this it? After everything she did for everyone. My dad never returned to carry his mum's coffin with my uncles. Six men carefully carried her up the stairs before two people opened the lobby doors. People ignorantly blocked the aisle. With organ music playing, I couldn't believe what I was seeing. Being under five feet tall, it only dawned on me when everyone parted like the sea. There were thousands of people crammed inside. Even the aisle was full, making it almost impossible to carry the coffin to the front of the church. Walking right behind, all I could do was look up at the bright chandeliers. After five steps, reality had hit home. I broke down, sobbing in tears uncontrollably. Sat on the front row, my body juddered up and down from

being unable to stop. My grandma's sister sat behind me and rubbed my shoulders trying to calm me down, as my uncle Kevin gave a brave speech on the podium. I was a complete wreck. Later on, we had to go to the crematorium. That was the worst day ever.

Weeks after the funeral, the inevitable happened. Like dying roots on a tree, the family fell apart. Various groups splintered off into smaller ones. Things would never be the same after that. My grandad was unchained with his drinking. The one person that controlled him was gone. Mick laid on his bed all day, refusing to go to work. Being a window cleaner, he lost all his customers due to his absence. My Uncle Kevin's wife started coming around to manage their finances. Not really caring about anything, my grandad and Mick later realised that money was going missing. Giving us spending money each week, she claimed that fifty pounds had vanished. The stupid bitch was blaming me. The accusation was unthinkable. To steal from my own family after everything they had done for me, was not once contemplated. She stood there in front of me with a smug look on her face. After she left, my uncle went to his room feeling that I betrayed him. The first thing I did was storm in his bedroom.

"You don't believe that load of lies, do you? I'd never steal from you."

"Well, I don't know who's took it."

Just before being accused, I had been out chasing a little shit that kept throwing stones at the front window. My loyalty was unquestionable. To serve the Army as a proud killing machine, ready to protect and die for my country was all I wanted to do. I wasn't about to turn into a coward like my dad, or a low life like my criminal associates. Years later it turned out she had been stealing from my grandad. It came as a shock to all of us. She was generally a nice woman that got on great with my gran, even working together at one stage. She was apart of the family for a long time. Holes started to appear in her character soon after. She was a chiseler that stopped working, built up huge debts to live a lazy lifestyle at home while getting fat. She had us all fooled as she laughed all day smoking. When she reached fifty many moons later, she died from a brain tumour. I got on with her good until she accused me. My dad used to fight with my Uncle Kevin when they were kids; that's the only explanation as to why he didn't like me. My dad must have kicked his ass. I never liked Kevin after he assaulted me. During my troublesome teens, I became disobedient for my gran. Kevin walked into Mick's room when I was watching his TV alone. He smacked me on the side of my head, then dragged me backwards. Once on my back, he sat on my neck with his knee and his two-year-old son in his arms. My cousin started crying as he watched it. Kevin threatened me with violence coming out with all sorts of shit. Only God knows what his problem was. He couldn't drink like my dad; two-pint champ. He was a stocky, muscular guy as well. My gran went

mad when she saw the red mark on my neck as I became teary in the kitchen. And to think I saved his son's life.

Not coping well, my family had fallen to pieces. At night time I wandered around the house taking a mental note of everything, reminiscing all the fantastic memories. Each corner of every room had a story to tell. "Thanks for everything Gran," I whispered to myself while I sat in her armchair with rays of light shining through gaps in the blinds from the street light. My time had come to an end in that house, so I left soon after. The atmosphere became too much for me. Deciding to separate myself, I went back to my mums away from the grief. On the way to the bus stop, the streets felt dark and empty. That was the loneliest walk of my life. It wasn't the right time to think about myself, but I couldn't help think about the implications of my future. My only lifeline was gone. Only she was the one that loved me enough to care, being the bastard son of two alcoholics. My mum's antics were just the start of it. It's all downhill from now on.

Chapter 7 - Love and beyond

Dossing around near mum's house, still listening to her shit every day with an empty fridge, Chris had managed to get his own house in Lostock Hall by his workplace. It was somewhere to crash on a sofa with a sleeping bag for the next few months. My life drifted with no real purpose. Nearly sixteen, I was almost able to claim benefits, while mum had pissed the last fifteen years up a wall. Losing some of her drinking money wouldn't have gone down too well. Not sitting my exams at school, I had no qualifications to my name. The only thing I learnt from school was the year of the Battle of Hastings. Chris didn't want me in the house all day using his electric, so I went to look for some kind of course. In Preston at a youth centre, a new course was available for young people. The Prince's Trust group was a three-month course where young people could learn life skills, build confidence, then help turn their life around. At that moment in time, it was the perfect opportunity and just what I needed. Located in Leyland, I even managed to get my childhood friend Tanya to join. Right off the bat, Monday to Friday was brilliant fun. Going out on day trips, and being part of a friendly group of people was a breath of fresh air. The team leader was a young woman named Lisa. Full of energy and always laughing, she made life worth living again.

When someone turns sixteen, they're supposed to have a massive birthday party. I didn't recall getting a card since my gran had passed. The £42 a week, was all I could expect once I claimed income support. £20 a week went to my brother's girlfriend for food, and the rest didn't go very far. Now and then I bought some weed, to try and lift me out of a depression that came and went. Everyone laughed at me.

"How can you be depressed, you're sixteen."

Tell that to my scared arms or the pain inside, I'd think to myself. In the mornings after leaving the house, I walked across the road to wait for the bus. Every morning at 8am, a girl around my age waited at the same bus stop. Stood on her left, each time she would look to the right, I would eye her up and down. She was the same height as me and looked sixteen. Wearing a blue apron, she must be on her way to work. I wished she was my girlfriend, but at that age, I wanted everyone to be my girlfriend. Her blonde hair was usually in a red or blue bobble. Not the slimmest girls, but certainly not fat, she looked a bit chubby. Whenever I looked to my left, I had the feeling she was checking me out, but I could be wrong. I'd never seen anyone so beautiful in my life. Being such a self-conscience and nervous person, approaching a girl directly was unheard of for someone like me. The bus arrived, so I extended my arm out like a gentleman to let her go first. There was nothing gentle about it; I just wanted to walk into her smell of perfume, while looking at her scrumptious bum. Weeks had past returning

to the same bus stop with perfect punctuality. All I wanted to do was talk to her. What if she had a boyfriend or thinks I'm stupid? I'd never be able to return to that bus stop ever again. She played on my mind all day. Not ready to leave my comfort zone, I never approached her. She was on my mind so much, I was driving Chris mad going on about her, and like he cared.

One Sunday returning back from my uncle's house, I walked in to find two young lads stood behind the three-seater settee. Not wanting to sit, they were talking to Chris and his girlfriend from behind them. One of the boys worked with Chris doing work experience. Sat quietly in the corner armchair, I gazed at the TV while they spoke to one another.

"Yeah, do you know that girl you keep talking about from the bus stop?"

Before even replying to what Chris just said, I looked straight at the two boys before he could say another word.

"Yeah, what about her."

"Well, this is her younger brother David and his cousin Ryan that I work with."

My chin hit the floor. I wanted the world to open up and swallow me. It was like a dream had come true. From that second on, I knew I had an indirect shot at the title. My heart raced leaving me with a dry mouth.

"You're her brother?"

Numb and barely unable to speak, it was a good job I was sat down as I readied myself for that one word he would surely tell me.

"What's her name?"

"Louise."

I looked at the floor and smiled momentarily. Finally, a name to go with that beautiful face I stood with every morning.

"Where does she live? Who does she live with? Has she got a boyfriend? What job does she have?"

Asking questions quicker than they could answer, I instantly made it clear how much I liked his sister. Not from my apparent interest in her, but because I blatantly told him "I fancy your sister." The odds of that situation must be a million to one; me being the million, Louise being the one. She worked in a flouriest during the summer, while being off college. She lived at home with her mum, stepdad, half-brother, and David. The best part was hearing she was single. Getting an insight into her life, it was sweet music to my ears.

"Why don't you phone her?"

"I don't have a phone."

"You can use mine if you want."

Bless David after receiving such advances from a stranger; he was willing to let me use his phone to catch her off guard. It was an unreal moment. I was so happy. They all egged me on

as I stayed in my seat thinking what to say. Once I had my story right, I walked into the next room to call her. My heart was in my mouth. Stood in total darkness, her name lit up in green on the phone as it rang. She answered thinking it was David.

"Hello."

"Hello is that Louise?"

"Who is it."

"I'm Joseph, the lad that stands at the bus stop with you in the mornings. Your brother knows my brother, and he let me use his phone to call you."

An awkward silence followed. The main artery in my neck pulsed down the phone, as I went bright red. At that point, there was no going back. If she said no, I will never return to that bus stop ever again.

"Erm... I thought it was David."

"I was just wondering if maybe you wanted to meet up one time."

We both went over again how I came into possession of David's phone. She seemed mystified.

"Well, I'm busy on Tuesday because I need to go to B&Q to buy a lamp for my art project, so maybe next week."

"Yeah that sounds good; I'll come with you."

"You want to come with me to buy a lamp? Next week would be better; I'm really busy."

"Honestly, I'd love to walk with you, even if it's for a short walk."

"You want to come to B&Q? I won't be able to stay out long."

My family knew all too well; if I want something, then I want it now. She gave in to my persistence and agreed to meet me in two days. Not really an ideal first date. After watching her for weeks, stood at that stupid bus stop, another second was too long. She laughed at my hastiness to meet so soon. It wasn't because I wanted sex, I was halfway in love with a girl I'd never even spoken to. Feelings came over me I'd never experienced before. The sensation made me feel warm inside. And so, the date was set; 8pm at the bus stop, on the 28th of August, 2001. Definitely, a date to remember.

Tuesday night couldn't come fast enough. Thank heavens she didn't get the bus on Monday morning; what an embarrassing moment that would have been. With an hour to go, the bathroom was mine. Shower, body spray, then gel in that order. My nerves kept strong until that gel went on. Butterflies in my stomach almost carried me down the stairs.

"Good luck."

My brother's girlfriend sniggered at me, almost laughing. Walking out of the house felt like entering death row. Only yards away, the bus stop was empty, giving me time to calm down. Not wanting to stand there, I did a lap around the block in one big circle. Nearing the bus stop after one lap, I

could see a girl in front of me with long blonde hair. Is that Louise? My eyes are bad. When she got to the bus stop, she disappeared around the side of it. Scared to death, I approached the corner like a police officer.

"Are you Louise!"

Stupidly commenting, it would have been some coincidence if it wasn't. What the hell was I saying. Gulps of air had made me feel dizzy. Stood in front of me was the most beautiful thing I had ever made eye contact with. Her blonde hair lit up the dark bus shelter, creating an aura that hypnotised me. Usually, her hair was tied up in the mornings. That night she let it down, every strand of hair stood on its own perfectly straight, flowing from side to side. She must have brushed and blow dried it for hours.

"Yes," she said smiling with her blue eyes, much bluer than mine.

"I walked around the block when I saw you weren't here."

"Really? I did the same."

A thin sheet of ice broke in my mind, while we laughed any nerves off. On the way, we exchanged questions about each other. I started with how her cousin worked with my brother, and how they came around on Sunday night. B&Q was over a mile away, so we had plenty of time to talk. We trailed through some kind of storm drain in the pitch black, barely big enough for the two of us. I couldn't believe she was about to make this walk alone, what a brave girl. Straight away it

was apparent she was mature, intelligent and gorgeous. She walked first into the store heading down the light aisle. Shining bright, she radiated in front of me, placing me into a trance. I couldn't take my eyes off her. Her project was to draw a lamp. Being left-handed, I could hardly write my name. On the way back, I insensitively asked her a stupid question. She would have told me in her own time, but I asked without thinking.

"How did you get that scar on your face."

"People always ask me that, just not as quick as you just did."

"Sorry. It doesn't change how you look; I just wondered how you got it."

"I ran into a glass door when I was a kid."

The scar went from the side of her nose, around her mouth and down to her chin. I felt like such an asshole for asking. She changed the conversation, asking if I knew any jokes.

"I know loads; I can't remember any apart from one. What do you call a prostitute with white eyes?"

"I don't know."

"Full."

She laughed her head off. It was a relief to amuse her. I wanted her to like me. When we got to the Labour club close to the bus stop, she insisted that I didn't walk her home. I wanted to see her home safe, but maybe she didn't want me

to know where she lived. Offering to walk her halfway, we agreed to go to hers.

"Stand at my back gate, while I drop my lamp off then I will walk back with you."

"Don't be stupid, I'll be fine on my own, you go in."

"No it's fine, I'll walk back."

Her house looked like it was in a nice area. We had walked across a field to get to hers. I couldn't believe how she walked through dark areas alone. Back to where we started, it was time to go our separate ways.

"Give me a hug then."

Not believing my luck, I was more than obliged. Under the street light, we wrapped our arms around each other's warm body. Her blonde fragranced hair brushed against my face, with my eyes closed. I needed that hug for sixteen years. Pulling back slowly, I wondered what she was doing before clicking on. Our cheeks rubbed past each other, only for our lips to connect, turning into a passionate snog. Cars driving passed pumped their horns, while two people came together. Resting my eyes, I savoured that kiss for as long as possible. Straight after, we walked in opposite directions with the promise to call one another. I was so happy and love-struck with an urge to scream at the top of my voice. When I got in, I sat with a stupid smile on my face for the rest of the night. It felt like it was meant it be. The following week or two, we stayed in touch over the phone, texting and ringing each

other on a temporary phone I got hold of. I just wanted to see her again as soon as possible, but she had loads of college projects to do at home. Meeting in the mornings must have been fate. Her job was only for a short time to fill a college break.

Louise and I had gained some trust and feelings for one another before she introduced me to her mum and stepdad. I'd also befriended David and his cousin, adding certainty that love might blossom. Another nervous moment, but good to be off the dark streets. A picture appeared in my mind of how her house looked inside, or what her mum was like. If she was anything like Louise, there would be nothing to worry about. We walked down a lane before entering her crescent. Modern detached buildings trailed around before reaching her suburban home. Intruding thoughts came over me. What if they don't like me? What if I don't stand up to their standards? When we got inside, her mother smiled at me and said hello. Her stepdad seemed nice as well. Her little brother laid on the floor watching TV as we all talked. Knowing what it's like to have a good family, I knew how to act. An ordinary family was all I wished for. How great it must be going home to a lovely house with loving people inside.

Staying with Chris was no different than being with my friends on the estate. Not having the same grandparents, he

had been around bad dudes all his life. Sat in the corner, all I could do was watch him play video games. It was surprising to let me stay in his home, given how tight and selfish he was. The only time he paid for anyone, was when he wanted to do something for himself. He never even shared a chocolate bar from a multipack in the cupboard. It was worse when his friends came around. Just when I thought our bad life was over, he brought some of his criminal friends around from where we just escaped. As they were in their mid-twenties, their stage in life was to drink and smoke weed every day. Doing what I did best, I went with the flow. They joked, blasting music whenever Chris hit the decks. Bobbing heads went to the sound of drum and bass, with swaying bodies like tough guys. Every conversation was about taking the piss out of everything, or who they had assaulted. My whole life was surrounded by those who would put everyone down, make fun or spot weaknesses. Who were they to judge anyone? That's where my insecurities came from, but being around those people made me feel safe. The second I was outside my comfort zone my life was a living hell. Each walk outside felt like the worst was going to happen. Being in such a predicament, if I went against the tide, I was in danger of being washed away. I wanted a life like my grandparent's or Louise. Being apart of a nuclear family in a decent place, was all I ever dreamt about. I would look through living room windows as I walked past imagining what kind of life the family inside had.

One night, Chris decided to record himself while he was drunk with his best friend, Toni. Toni was a bit of a tough guy that smoked weed all day, throwing his weight around with his train wreck of a life. The two of them together became pretty wild. I respected how he had my back still, whenever I needed someone sorting out.

"If anything should ever happen to me, I want the whole world to know that Joseph ate shit. He ate it when he was a baby, and I caught him."

They were both in hysterics. If only he knew what memory needed to exist. I knew the truth. My photographic memory remembered everything from the age of four. I was so traumatised watching my parents fight in pubs, as I clutched tightly to my teddy bear. I took pleasure from having a good look at their pathetic life, and the direction it was going in. Thank God I met Louise, what a blessing in disguise. My time in that house with Chris and his girlfriend was no sweet lullaby. His long-term girlfriend enjoyed taking the piss out of me or making me act like her skivvy. Chris, on the other hand, was narcissistic, self-centred, and very controlling. In simple terms, he was a real asshole sharing a third of mum's personality. Both of them together were a match made in heaven. She would bow and serve his every need, even though she lost her family over him. Then he would cheat on her, before coming clean and she still stayed with him. It drove me mad how they treat me. I wanted to smash the house up. Being scared of Chris, there was no way I'd say

anything. Not unless I wanted to be on the street. On occasions, I would sneak off to the bathroom upstairs. Grabbing a razor once I took my clothes off, I sliced across my chest. Every slice released a small amount of pressure from within, better than any acupuncture. Putting up with their shit was not so bad, sat with a bleeding chest that felt like I had Vicks on. A murderous rage was slowing boiling away deep inside me, the older I got. Only love could save me.

Visiting Louise's house the first few times, we had to sit in the kitchen. Her mum knew we'd be sexually active, but it was only until they got to know me. In my opinion, I was a good kid with a lost cause. Later, we started going up to her room. Her mum figured that as long as her daughter was indoors, she was safe. As for sex, well, if Louise were going to do it, she would find a way like any other teenager on the planet. Her room was small, making way for her brothers in the bigger room. The first thing I noticed was a painting on her wall.

"Please Lord, if you can't make me skinny, then make all my friends fat."

A giant pig covered her wall behind a green background. I got the impression she was insecure about her weight. She wasn't even fat. I didn't care if she had three arms, and one leg; to me, she was the most beautiful girl I'd ever seen. Having a bunk bed with storage space underneath, there was

barely enough room to stand by the door. We climbed the ladder to sit on her bed. It was cramped which meant I could get closer to her. She seemed embarrassed. It was the perfect nest for two love birds. I was sat on a bed next to the girl of my dreams, still amazed how this moment came to be. We had to lean over to watch her small television, but most of the time we sat at each end of the bed talking. Having our legs between each other, we started leg wrestling and tickling each other's feet after getting on like a house on fire. Lying beside one another, we passionately kissed until we needed a glass of water. We took it slow for the first few weeks. Each visit seemed more intense. Mounting her, we held tightly with our fully clothed bodies. After working up a sweat, the heat had nowhere to go being so close to the ceiling. The window was too small to expel the kind of heat we produced. Taking it a little bit further, the kissing started to turn each other on. Rubbing up and down, we masturbated one another using our crotch. I had to press harder with the jeans she wore. With her mum and stepdad downstairs, there was no way we could get undressed. Once we calmed down, we talked about the first time we ever clapped eyes on each other.

"Every time you looked away, I was staring at you."

"Seriously, that's what I did. I looked at you thinking; he's hot."

We froze looking deep into each other's blue eyes before kissing. From that moment I wanted to spend the rest of my life with her.

"Louise, home time."

Her mum shouted from the bottom of the stairs. We pushed the limits to see how much extra time we could get before her mum shouted for a second time. Walking through the living room towards the back door, I smiled and said goodbye to her mother. If only my mum turned out like that. Outside we had a quick chat, a kiss, and a cuddle before she had to go back inside. We had only known each other for a few weeks. The thought of losing her at this stage would be disastrous for me.

"I know I've not known you long, but…. will you start seeing me."

"I don't know; I've been hurt by my ex-boyfriends in the past."

They must have been losers if they couldn't see what a great girl she was.

"I'd never hurt you, Louise; You're the nicest girl I've ever met. I promise I won't hurt you if you give me a chance."

I made a promise I knew I couldn't keep knowing what a screw-up I was. After a few minutes, she gave me an answer.

"OK then."

I knew she wanted the same. She didn't want to give her heart away so easily. If I didn't capture her heart when I did, someone else could of. Once I exited through her back gate onto a large football pitch, the night sky was clear with a full moon in front. Looking up, I smiled at the perfectly round shape. Taking a deep breath, that was the happiest feeling I'd experienced. My stomach felt like it didn't exist, while my heart and lungs felt like one big air bubble. Joy lifted me high up as I danced across the field, kicking an imaginary football into the nets. "She's mine!" Life was about to get a whole lot better. All my life seemed to do with itself was balance down a thin line of good and evil, poverty and wealth. Sooner or later, that balance had to tip in one direction.

Walking into Chris's house, everyone was transfixed to the television.

"Have you seen the news? Two planes have just flown into the twin towers in New York."

Blood left my face seeing the two buildings on fire. While I was falling in love, Terrorist had attacked America, prompting an inevitable war. Innocent people jumped from way up in the clouds to avoid the fire. The horror show unfolded with each building collapsing. It was the most frightful thing I had ever seen. My ambition to live in America was undeterred. That night I prayed for the victims before climbing into my sleeping bag. It made me appreciate life that little bit extra

Every day after becoming a couple, Louise and I tried to see each other seven days a week. The strong, urging connection pulled us tightly together. We longed for each other's company once apart, becoming infatuated with each other. My brother's house was not ideal, so we headed to hers all the time. Her mum didn't mind. Every night after tea and once our daily activities were finished, I walked to meet her by the shops. The walk to hers was the best part of the day. Holding hands, we shared stories of what we had got up to. She anaesthetised me with words. Her body carried me with hers. Her soft subtle hand released any pain, fear or discomfort I had in my heart. The world could be on fire around me, and I wouldn't notice. A growing vine of peace overtook any doubt in my life. Her mouth, her kiss, her indescribably soft lips seized my soul. The road ahead lead me to a blessed garden of freedom. Looking forward to being alone, a month had passed our newly found relationship. Unexpectedly, no one ever came into her room when we were alone. We kissed each other for what felt like hours. If we could have crawled into each other's bodies, I'm sure we would have. Lying on her back in her yellow polo top, I pulled away from a kiss keeping full eye contact. She unfastened her jeans, signalling she was ready. Lifting her bum, I slowly pulled them off placing each hand on her cold-inner thighs, running my palms with hard skin up towards her hips. Our eye contact broke momentarily as my eye's fixed between her legs. Leaning my head to one side, I slid

my tracksuit pants down, positioning my knees before closing the humid gap. The kissing alone starved any oxygen above us. Still half dressed in case her mum walked in, I penetrated her enough to become one. Our tongues swirled together as we mixed like two colours of paint, embracing what was set to be love. Sweat poured off us during her orgasm, leaving me to cum inside her. Lying in that position locked together forever was never going to be. A thud came upstairs, causing us to return to an upright position. It was a false alarm; someone needed the bathroom. Louise opened the small window wide, spraying any perfume to rid the smell of sex. Later, she laid on my chest by the window, as a cool breeze flowed down our necks, gradually cooling us down. The entire world outside that bedroom door was irrelevant. Everything I needed was in that room. The remaining hour went too fast before going home for the night. At the back door, we gave each other a tight cuddle. She happily smiled as I walked away. Words were not needed to communicate. The clear, chilly night waited for me to cross the field. The moon pierced my eyes, imprinting the memory of what just happened. It was the night I fell madly in love with Louise.

Saturday nights became my favourite. Louise was left to babysit her younger brother, while her mum and stepdad went to the labour club for a few drinks. The cupboards got raided, the living room was ours, and we could do whatever

we wanted. As soon as the parents left, it was clothes off, and straight into the shower together to make love. The shower rained down her back, while I rubbed shower cream around her perfect breast, sucking her tongue. We laughed and smiled looking down each others nose, in moments of ecstasy. Ending up on her mum's bed, we carried on making love better than married couples. Before going back downstairs, we paused on the landing for a cuddle.

"I need to tell you something." She said hiding her face.

"I need to tell you something as well."

"You go first."

"haha, no, you go first."

Shying away from me, I encouraged her to tell me first. I had a feeling what she wanted to say.

"I think I've fallen in love with you."

Talking down into my jumper, I lifted her face by her chin with her puppy dog eyes looking up at me.

"Louise... I've fallen in love with you as well. I fell in love the first moment I saw you."

Once downstairs, I laid behind her on the sofa taking full advantage of what married life must feel like. The possibilities of two people being in love at the same time were astronomical. Adults called it a cute relationship, yet they had never truly been in love. Chris and his girlfriend didn't know the meaning; neither did my mum. Not one

person around me had ever made love; if they did, they wouldn't be assholes all their life. I felt like a God at sixteen. Still, I pitied them for not experiencing such a wonder. Suddenly, I had the edge over everyone. With Louise beside me, I could achieve anything.

The situation at my brothers stayed the same for months. My course ended, leaving the perfect time frame to start the same college as Louise. Any extra time with my love was all that entered my mind. Going into her second year being such a good prospect, the only course available to me was the silly class. Full of reprobates and disabled people, the college knew we were unemployable. If any of us proved by the end of the year that we were capable, the next year would be a Maths and English course. In simple terms, it would take six to eight years in college to reach the level Louise was at. She was heading for success, while I headed for the toilet. Not sitting my exams left me screwed. It was only a matter of time before we parted. There was no way I could drag her down, yet I couldn't let go. Successfully entering my course, me and Louise met every morning to get the same college bus. Meeting that same smile every day was the only purpose I needed to wake up. Sat on the bus at the back with Louise and her friends, the conversation came up about someone's broken nose. I tried to join the conversation to take an active interest.

"I've broken my nose twice," I said to her friends.

"I can tell," the girl replied as everyone laughed.

"Louise has gone bright red, haha." Her friend pointed out.

There wasn't one point of entry in a society where I could fit. It always felt like looking through a window. No matter how I acted, or what I said, people would still consider me as a chav or a nobody. Even if they had to put a front on, it was clear what they thought. A leopard can't change its spots, so I wear them proudly. Fuck the haters, and wave bye to the do-gooders, because one day I will go down with the ship as a product of society.

Meeting some cool friends, we knew where we belonged; at the end of the college where no one goes. The tutors seemed nice. They put us to work building public footsteps with stone and wood. Like a chain gang along a US highway, I pushed wheelbarrows full of stone three times my weight. Getting more than we bargained for, the college course turned into slavery, believing it's what we needed. Hard work was all my grandad ever raved about, and look how narrow-minded he turned out. Finding Louise during short breaks was something I looked forward to. Living different lives, we never mixed with each other's friends. We couldn't keep our hands off each other, she was irresistible. Once or twice, we sneaked into the college toilets when it was quiet. She would give me a blowjob before bending her over in a cubicle, while students came and went without knowing what we were up to. It was thrilling living on the edge of life. We couldn't even

wait to get home. Arriving late one morning, my classroom was empty. Everyone had already set off to re-build half of Leyland. The news went down well, knowing I missed it. When I found Louise, I took her to my quiet classroom for some privacy. She was sat on the desk where I worked while I stood up kissing her.

"Shall we have sex?"

"Are you kidding, what if your class comes back?"

"They won't come back until 3pm."

"Someone could walk in though."

"Well, that's a risk worth taking," I said to her.

We pulled our pants down and made love on the classroom table. It was right next to the staff room as well. The door had a small window to look through, but being on a bend, a teacher would have to approach the door to look through. A student or a teacher could walk in any second. Consequences didn't enter our mind, only love. Thank god no one did. What an embarrassing moment that would have been; her tutor explaining to her mum that she was kicked out of an A-level art class for having sex in a classroom. Our sex life definitely became kinkier. It was a stupid thing to do, but love blinded us.

Not having any sexy lingerie of her own, she improvised. On Saturday night having the house to our self, she started wearing her mum's lingerie. Lying on top of her mum's bed

with the lights on, we made love in front of the large mirrors. I couldn't help but laugh when she wasn't looking. The only thing missing was the cameraman. The thought of her mum finding out was unthinkable. We knew how to push the limits. After tidying the bed, I dropped the condom on the floor by accident. The last thing anyone wanted was pregnancy at sixteen.

"For god sake, don't forget to get rid of that; my mum will kill me."

"I won't don't worry."

After getting a shower, it was home time before her parents got back. The next day I returned after eating my Sunday dinner. Louise met me at the back door with a distressed look on her face.

"My mum wants a word with us both."

"Why what's up?"

"I don't know."

We took guesses at what she wanted. We feared that her little brother grassed us up for using her bed. Then she came outside nearly whispering.

"What do you think you are both doing in my room. You two are disgusting. I found a condom on the floor by my bed last night. What if your stepdad found it? He would have gone ballistic. I appreciate you both practising safe sex, but don't ever go in my room again."

Her face was bright red from pushing out a quiet scolding. I speak for Louise when I say that we both wanted to die from shame. Her mum roasted us alive. Just when we thought we were invincible; an adult would come along to bring us back to reality. It didn't stop us of course. Her mum would need a stick to separate us. After that, we just climbed in her mum's bed instead so it didn't crease the bed covers. Lou's room was too small for the sexual positions we wanted to try.

Knowing my life was on borrowed time like my grandad always said, old habits had stayed with me whatever I did. College became a drag, so I started to take cannabis with me. Unable to smoke it, I nibbled on the brown resin like a mouse until I felt stoned. Walking the corridors made me anxious and tense. Large crowds of normal people were not my thing. Any sense of normality became hard to cope with. Although I had the girl of my dreams, my future was bleak. Being realistic and somewhat bright, there was no way I could deal with responsibility. Wanting to block everything out pulled me in one direction, while expectations pulled me in another. On a waiting list for a flat, Chris wanted me to move out when a place became available. I wasn't ready to face my trauma, grow up, then suddenly become a responsible adult. Inside I was in pieces, and not one person knew. On top of my dilemma, my hormones were all over. Louise was the same with her hormones. After going to the doctor for a problem she had, they prescribed her with Co-

proxamol; a strong pain killer. Once she told me, I started taking them, swallowing half at a time. The feeling was like being on a cloud. Having fifty in her room, I took thirty home to help me get through any college anxieties. Just before the bell at dinner, I would swallow half, turning into a numb student. The feeling was great; no more pain or suffering, just a calm atmosphere. That, mixed with the resin I chewed on throughout the day, left me on cloud nine. Being drunk on love and substances, I fell towards the void I'd been searching for.

Being under the influence, my behaviour spiralled out of control. Losing the capability to differentiate reality from a dream, each day became harder to function. Acting irrational followed from such a foggy mind, causing me to think that nothing in the world had ever mattered. Every breath I had taken was nothing more than a big joke. I became so withdrawn, Louise seemed a million miles away. One of the girls from my class took advantage of my altered state of mind, by coming on to me. I'd never even spoken to her before, yet she was all over me in the recreation room, where people ate their food. She was nothing but a low-class slag, not even in the same league as Louise. Numb from any emotion or feelings, I didn't stop her advances when she was kissing my neck. I could have been beaten, robbed or sexually abused without a care in the world. No one could harm me anymore. Unknowingly not myself, I was betraying

the person that gave me love, attention and all the time in the world. To me, it was Thursday; I was entirely out of it like a zombie. Addicted to tablets and weed, I fed my habit without a second thought. Louise had finally seen enough. She could have walked away an left me. Instead, she saved me. During a dinner break, she stormed into the recreational room. First, she grabbed the slag off me then hit her, threatening to kill her if she goes near me again. Then, she picked up the full can of coke I had in front of me and poured it all over my head. Everyone watched the commotion as Louise baptised me. I was at the bottom of the lake again in Florida, when Louise reached down and pulled me to the surface. The light in the ceiling was mistaken for the sun. My true love had become the Virgin Mary. The crowd around us represented the children of God. Gasping for air when I reached the top, I was reborn again with clarity. Watching Louise walk off down the corridor after regaining my senses, I chased after her. That was the biggest mistake of my life. In a moment of selfishness to escape reality like my mum and dad, I had destroyed the purity of love we had. I had poisoned the well I drank from. A ripple effect that day forward caused us both to collide like two neutron stars.

Louise's Achilles' heel was her temper. Not only was she the brightest pupil at her school, but she was also the toughest. She certainly knew how to punch. The love we had evolved into an obsession for each other. Spending too much time

turned us against one another. Once two energies realise they can't form as one, they either bounce off each other or explode on impact. We did both. Arguments of paranoia about our exes turned violent. I never had a fight in my life. Unable to control her emotions, she punched me in my already broken nose. Another time she punched me in the ribs causing a fracture. Most girls slapped at the worst. We wrestled and fought each other halfway down the street on a bad day, with onlookers amazed. I tried not to physically hurt her. Half the time I was fending her off me. Being bigger than me, it was hard to gain control of her once she got going. I tried everything. If there was one person that can light someone's fuse, it's me. At one stage, I encouraged her to hit me if it made her feel better. We held on for dear life trying to harness the power of love. A mighty power flowed through my veins. The only foreseeable outcome seemed to be death. The pitfall had revealed itself. The relationship was flawed. We had to die together or be pulled apart forever. Coming to a sudden end, my substance abuse ended moments after Louise slammed me into a college advertising board. Unbearable pain in my stomach left me cramped on the floor like I had been stabbed. The fighting had to wait for a moment. Coincidently being next to the nurse's office, I had to come clean with what substances I had been taking if she was going to help me.

"You have an ulcer in your stomach from taking Co-proxamol. You must stop taking them immediately. Take this yellow tablet, and the pain will go away."

Already back to reality from the drink over my head, and being thrown into a wall, the magic pill stopped the pain. Having gone through thirty, I never touched another tablet. It came to a dramatic end when I walked across a field by the college and fell to my knees during a breakdown. My love followed me in tears as we held each other on the grass. How did it get this?

Winter settled in signalling Christmas around the corner. The freezing cold weather brought Lou and me together again. Helping her deliver Avon catalogues, we cherished every moment from one extreme to another. Her crescent lit up with a white layer of snow. We laughed trying to prop each other up, slipping and sliding across ice landing on our ass. On Christmas day, I took advantage of two dinners at each house. It was the first Christmas without my gran. I felt selfish in love when my family was going through a bad time. If alive, the whole family would be sharing presents sat on chairs that went around the living room. I also wouldn't have met Louise, so I was torn between the two aspects. Babysitting on New Year's Eve, we cuddled on the sofa in each other's arm when the Big Ben clock tower struck midnight. Turning back towards me, we kissed well into the firework display on TV, with our favourite song playing on the kitchen stereo; Barthezz - on the move. 2002 brought a nervous feeling of "what's in store for me this year." Not wishing to continue with my dead-end college course, we

both talked about dropping out. She found her art class difficult. I found it hard to believe because she was a great artist, even taking up photography. Her mum found it suspicious leaving at the same time. I wanted her to continue. Already feeling responsible for her decision, I knew her mum held me accountable. My ship was going down anyway, the last thing I wanted was for her to join me. She planned to find work instead. That was easy for her to say with the qualifications she had. The last thing I wanted to do was work. Life was terrifying enough. Working as a cleaner for £4 an hour was not worth getting out of bed, even if I wasn't screwed up. Joining the Army seemed unlikely. I was underweight and had a criminal record with fines to pay for the next five years.

Halfway through January relaxing with Louise after making love in her bed, knowing no one would walk in, I received a phone call. My mum phoned out of the blue. It must be important if she's ringing. Giving a shit about me was not on her to-do list.

"Joseph, it's mum. You need.... You need to... come here... quickly, something has happened."

She was sobbing like a baby. I couldn't be bothered with her silly games, so I demanded she told me over the phone.

"Just... get here as soon as you can."

"If I come all the way down in a taxi for no reason, I will never talk to you again."

I hung up to her snivelling down the phone. She was drunk as usual, but something was wrong. Around the time I usually left Lou's to go home, she walked into her mum's dark bedroom to ask if she could come with me for an hour. After agreeing, we both jumped in a taxi. Angry at what all the fuss was about, my response to her calling was half-hearted. We walked in to find her sobbing in the living room. Levi was nowhere to be seen.

"I... I... can't..."

"If you don't tell me in thirty seconds I'm walking out!"

"The police... have been... your... your dad is dead."

"My real dad?"

"Yeah...he's..he's....dead."

Louise and I looked dazed at each other. I sat on the stairs taking in what she just said. We didn't hang around, so we left. My mum was no use to me after that. Not knowing where to go, we walked into town. A police van pulled up next to me with no intention to run like I once did.

"Are you Joseph?"

The policewoman knew who I was. I'd been stopped and searched by most of the police force for the last six years. The second she said my name I broke down, turning away in tears.

"Look after him will you, make sure he gets home."

"I will, thanks, bye."

Needing to get back home, we both walked to the train station so Louise could jump in a black cab.

Stood alone on the dark empty streets, I needed to get to my grandad's to tell him his son was dead. My dad had the courtesy to put my mum down as his next of kin. The only person that needed to know if something happened to him was me. Walking so slow towards Fulwood, it took an hour. Entering through the back door, my grandad sat in his usual spot drinking beer and whiskey. Stood with tears in my eyes, I broke the news to him.

"My dad has died."

"Your dad has died? who told you that?"

"The police and my mum. You need to ring the family."

"Do you know what time it is? It's eleven thirty at night."

Am I going insane, or am I the only one that gave a shit about life? He didn't bat an eyelid. Walking upstairs, I opened Mick's door turning his light on.

"Mick, wake up. My dad's dead."

He questioned how I knew, confirming adults don't listen to what young people have to say. Walking downstairs with him, he confronted my grandad.

"Right, get on the phone and find out what's going on, don't just sit there."

"Do you know what time it is."

"Who gives a shit about time. Your son has just died; do you not understand that."

They both argued, so I walked out. It became clear what my grandad thought about his own son. As well as being a drunk, he hated niggers and queers; his own words.

Later that week, my uncles and I along with his shady wife drove to Bournemouth in a van to get his stuff. I don't know why she came; my dad never had any money. I had to sit in the back of a windowless van for six hours on a chair like an immigrant. One of dads friends met us outside his flat to let us in. Not seeing many of his friends before, you could tell the bloke was gay. He was as camp as a row of tents. My dad's gay life that he hid so well revealed itself. He threw all my dad's empty bottles, removing any gay porn before we arrived, and any other weird shit. None of us wanted any embarrassment. Presuming he had drunk himself to death, we had to wait for his autopsy report. Behind his door was a pile of letters piled up high. It was two weeks after his 40th birthday when he died; what a waste. I never bothered to send him a card. He was too selfish to care. Not being seen for days, one of the neighbours placed a ladder against his bedroom window. My dad was found dead on top of his bed

with the window open. Entering his flat, the first thing that hit me was the stench of death. It was a smell I will never forget. In the microwave was half a bowl of beans. He sold everything to live off beans and cider until he died. The coroner sat in the living room with my family, discussing what happens next. Stood by the doorway, I broke down in tears. Mick took me for a walk to calm me down past a car garage that sold Porsche's. Returning to the flat, I sat on his bed where he died. What have you gone and done now dad, I thought to myself. Then I went through all his clothes in the wardrobe, placing his jumpers to my face. His smell was still present in his clothing. Once the van was filled with his stuff, we took a good look around before returning to Preston. I was now the new owner of his motorbike leathers and his real tiger skin.

Dad died from bronchopneumonia; pneumonia in his lungs that could have been treated with antibiotics, according to my doctor. Drinking would have killed him regardless. My prediction never to see him again came true. His funeral was held in Bournemouth a week later. Neither happy in Preston or Bournemouth, it didn't matter where he was cremated. I didn't decide to view his body in the morgue. Mick said he had a beard, and looked gaunt. Always clean shaven, it was hard to picture. There was no way I was about to have that image stuck in my head forever. I didn't go to his funeral. He caused enough damage. I don't see how I should suffer any

more after the mess he left before running off. His ashes were returned to me, his only child. It weighed a ton as well.

"When I die, put me in a black bin bag, then throw me into the sea."

My dad sure did have a way with words, as my mum did. Not knowing what to do with them, he would have been happy for me to throw them in a bin. Mick and I went to our family grave. With around four relatives in the same spot, I dug a small hole with my hands. Pouring his ashes into the ground, a strong gust of wind blew his remains all over my face and in my mouth! Not only did he walk out on me, but now I had his ashes all over me.

"Fuck sake.... Thanks, dad."

With January down the sinkhole, the rest of the year had concerned me. Eleven more months of uncertainty would surely take shape. With my gran and dad dead within twelve months, it was a hard time. My break came when a flat near Chris became available. I'd not slept in a bed for nearly a year. Louise was as happy as I was; our own space. The first thing I did was try to get her to move in. Knowing how volatile the relationship had become, he mum refused and rightly so. Owning my dad's microwave and a small television, I didn't have a penny to my name. The government gave me £300 to decorate and buy what I needed. By the time I had purchased everything for the

kitchen, there was no money left. The flat had no carpets or curtains, so I decided to live in the bedroom with bed sheets against the window. My Uncle Kevin helped me take my bed from my grandad's to the new flat. It was nice being alone for the first hour, then it feels like being on a desert island. No one visited apart from Louise. Even Chris couldn't be bothered to look at my flat. Lou and I enjoyed having total privacy. My first official night, we both got naked while she laid on her belly as I massaged her back. The tension I was releasing was temporary. The real pressure was building from being in that flat without boundaries. Being in public or at her mum's had toned us both down during bad arguments. Now totally alone, we had no safeguard.

With long days pacing up and down my flat, the situation was shit. I sat on my window ledge in the living room with nothing but wooden floorboards. The feeling of loneliness was scary. Now working, Louise went through life without speedbumps. It was good for some positivity to come out of the situation. Her mind was all over the place coming to see me. Three or four visits later, we ended up arguing again. Arguments turned into violence. Presuming she was still messed up over what I did in college, her punches rained down, while I slapped, wrestled, and gently punched her back. Stood in the kitchen on her own during a breather, she grabbed a large kitchen knife from out of the sink. There was so much drama; she left the flat crying with the knife. I kept

ringing her to come back, while her emotions drove her mad. Within an hour, she had returned in the same state. Having the knife returned to the sink, we ended up wrestling on my bed. I had gotten on top of her, completely pinning her down. That was my first time overpowering her, but it didn't work. Still going apeshit, there was a plate next to her head with a butter knife on it. Out of ideas, I grabbed the knife and put it to her neck thinking she would snap out of it, from how serious the situation was getting. That didn't work, so I left her to do whatever she wanted. She ran out of my flat in a right state. Twenty minutes later she started texting me.

"I'm sat on the train line; I don't want to live anymore."

Immediately getting my shoes on, I ran to the local platform knowing she meant it. Unable to see her, I ran to the next platform close to her house. She was sat on the train line crying with her head in her hands. It killed me to see her so upset. I tried to drag her off the line, but she was too heavy for my weak arms, exhausted from all the wrestling we had just done.

"I want to kill myself; get off me."

"No, you are not, get off the line now before a train comes."

With trains every half hour, there was bound to be one due. Pulling with all my strength, I managed to get her off. She stormed home in a complete wreck. I backed off hoping she would calm down before getting home. It reminded me of the

time my mum tried to kill herself by jumping in a ditch. I had to drag her back in the car.

Getting back to my flat, I fell asleep after all the madness. By tea time, someone was banging on the front door that woke me up. Ignoring it the first time, I crept around trying to figure out what was going on. With nowhere to escape living in an upstairs flat, I was trapped. Fifteen minutes later, my door was being banged and kicked.

"Who is it?"

"Open this door now, or I'll break it down."

It was her biological father in a foul mood. Being known for a nut-case, me and Lou went to loads of pubs with him at the weekends, while he put on a karaoke. Always facing danger, I opened the door to him. The crazy bastard jumped on me, as I covered my head with my arms.

"If you ever touch Louise again, I will fucking kill you. Don't ever go near her again. I'm the hardest man in Leyland; I bite peoples noses off."

Shaking on my back against the stairs, all I could do was wait for it to be over. It was a relief when he left. I couldn't believe the love of my life had turned it all against me. I could see where she got her anger. The following ten minutes concluded with my decision to go back to my mums. Louise was gone, Chris was a waste of time, and my flat had nothing inside it anyway. I'd rather suffer at my mums; at least I felt

alive instead of being alone. Angry, I smashed her £300 phone up, then ripped all the photos we took together. We couldn't accept that fact that we had ex-partners. We couldn't stand anyone looking at each other. Leaving the keys, the flat sat empty until the council took over it again. Being so angry, I didn't want to see her ever again. I took betrayal very serious, even if I was a hypocrite.

Two weeks later, her brother David knocked on my mum's door.

"Louise is sat on the park; she needs to see you."

"I don't want to see her, tell her to go home."

Her family stopped us being together. The relationship was doomed. Ten minutes later, he knocked again.

"She really wants to see you; she's stood over there by that ally."

Walking over with him, I could see she was crying. Leaving us to talk, I listened to what she had to say.

"I'm so sorry Joseph; I didn't mean to hurt you. It's killing me not being able to see you."

"You should have thought about that before telling your dad."

It all unfolded when I left her to go home from the train station. Collapsing on the floor, she had phoned her dad's girlfriend, where she went on to tell her dad. Siding with his

daughter, there was no way my story mattered. Not caring what she did wrong, my love for her was written in stone. I placed my arms around her as she wept.

"I just need you to tell me that everything is going to be OK Joseph."

"It will don't worry. I'm right here. Calm down."

We knew it was damaged. No one could come between what we had. Pulled together by the power of love, we let an unseeable force move us like puppets. Coming to Preston to work, we used that to be able to meet up. Some of her relatives worked in town as well, so we had to be careful. At midnight twice a week, I walked over four miles to meet her outside her house. Once we met up, we walked back to my mums. Leaving her house every day before her mum woke up, her absence was never noticed. We spent the night together in my bed before she left for work. The plan was sweet. Making love was that extra bit special. Her family gave her an ultimatum; them or me. She wanted me but needed them. We held on before inevitably being torn apart. With pressure from every angle, my mum was back to being a dick, kicking me out for smoking weed, or having my girlfriend around. Like she was any better than me. I applied for a hostel straight away. Getting my flat was fortunate, but it's not what I needed. Surviving on and off the streets, only God could help me now. To my amazement, he answered my prayer. The council phoned me with an interview at a hostel, right next to the town centre. It was amongst all the smack-

head-hotels, but that didn't matter. My best friend from high school lived around the corner in a pub. After my interview, the support worker that did the night shift instantly knew I needed help. Before finishing my story of what kind of life I had, they cut it short, showing me to my new room. Now impossible to spend time with Lou, we drifted apart. The hostel declined any visitors. We met a few times, finding public places to have sex, but it wasn't the same. She deserved Better. I was never in her league to start with.

Chapter 8 - Hostels Galore

Following the staff member, we walked upstairs to the third floor. Because I was new, I had to take the small room up in the heavens. If someone moved out, eventually I could work my way down to bigger rooms. It was tiny. Just enough space for a bed and a wardrobe. With no money or food, the staff gave me two cheap loaves of bread, and three bottles of Lipton ice tea to last me for two weeks. I don't even know how I survived before next payday. Sipping on that disgusting drink I'd never heard of, I used it to wash the dry bread down. Needing it to last, I rationed each day. Being at mum's didn't get me much more than what I had in that room, so surviving off bread and liquids was nothing new. My tolerance for ignoring hunger was second nature. Every tenant in that place was vulnerable like me. The word "vulnerable" made me laugh. I was vulnerable as a child; now I'm used, abused and flushed down the toilet. Mixing with the rest of the idiots in that place, I soon lost all hope on life. All of them sneaked cannabis, tablets and alcohol inside the hostel, to get smashed every day. I was trying to avoid the path our parents lead us down, while they embraced it. Not seeing a way forward with a heavy heart, I started to drink vodka. I met a new friend that lived on my floor, a Muslim lad who escaped a dangerous situation of his own. He called me "Bunty" for some reason whenever he saw me with a smile. I wasn't old enough to buy alcohol, but he was. He went a few times before it turned into a daily habit. I only

bought quarter sized bottles, but it was enough to get around my thin body fast enough. There was nothing else to do. My family did the same, maybe I was the missing link that needed to follow suit. I didn't want to live anymore, wishing I was dead.

Back to a place within my head that I hated, two of the girls in the hostel started to come on to me. Being a good-looking lad, there was never a shortage of attention. I strangely had no attraction to any other girl after falling in love. It was weird. Even when they threw themselves at me, there was no interest from my part whatsoever. Being drunk one night in the lounge, one of the girls had left love bites all over my neck. Trying to claim me, it didn't work.

"Louise is going to kill me."

Worried about what she would think, I tried to cover them up. Two days later she came to visit me with a new cap on my seventeenth birthday. My heart sank when she noticed them. I didn't even kiss any girls, they just seemed to climb all over me every time I was off my face. She walked off ending the relationship. Without defending myself, there was nothing I could do. My birthday was not worth celebrating. The worst present ever was the loss of my girlfriend. Homeless, surrounded with parasites, there was no chance for me now. I couldn't go any lower in society. Arms pulled me down into hell, as Louise's hand slipped away forever. Everyone had abandoned me. My family presumed I had a normal life,

calling me a lazy bastard for not going to work. If only they knew the half of it. I knew where I stood in society, but even a rat doesn't abandon its family. The hostel was a large building, chopped into rooms. Girls lived downstairs, the guys lived upstairs. Not everyone was bad, some were just kicked out by their parents, impatiently waiting for them to turn sixteen; bastards. The staff room was by the front door, with 24-hour staff working to support and watch the CCTV. Most of us took turns to talk to the staff members all day. It was good to relax in a room around adults that listened to us with a cup of tea. Being unbiased without judgement, they helped us without our knowing.

Alcohol didn't have the effect I wanted. It just added fuel to my rage tank to the point of overflow. My inverted anger became a pressure cooker. Feeling imprisoned in my room with nothing but hatred for the world, I returned to self-harm. I wanted to destroy someone. Drinking miserably in such a weak mental state, my personality reflected my mum. Pulling a razor out with my top off, I sliced across my stomach and chest. Being angry and drunk, the razor went deeper than previously. Staring at myself in the mirror, I couldn't see my eyes, I saw my mothers. Lit brightly green, monstrous eyes glared back at me. Blood had turned my whole body red, with no skin visible. Taking two fingers, I dapped the blood from my body to camouflage my face. It was time for war. I was ready to kill. Pouring vodka into my

bright green eyes, no one could reach me now. Coming of age, the time to stand up to all this fucking shit was now. One of the girls knocked on my door. Ready for war, I ran over the trench towards anyone stood in my way. The door opened.

"Oh my god! – Joseph, what the hell are you doing?"

Looking through her, the wall looked back at me.

"Nothing is wrong, just leave me alone."

Her voice temporarily snapped me out of the craziness. My life went on like that for a while. Even the weakest people can become dangerous when backed into a corner.

Heading towards destruction, I linked up with the bad lads in the hope for trouble, but it never came. I knew I was better than that. Letting go of myself was letting everyone else win. At night, I sat with a young couple that was homeless on the street. The girl had lived in the hostel, but decided to live rough to stay with her boyfriend. Coming out of prison, he knew how to hotwire cars. After trying to convince him to show me, he threatened to kick my ass if I stole a car. During the day, I walked into one of the smack-head-hotels out of curiosity with an associate. Rooms sat empty with rubbish and needles all over the floor. Not really knowing much about hard drugs, it was interesting to see how people lived. Stepping over syringes was like walking through a minefield. How someone could use so many was beyond me. One wrong

step balancing over them was likely to result in one of us contracting HIV. That hotel was probably my next destination if I didn't gain control of myself. Other times I rode a bike through town dressed in all black, with my hood up. Ignoring commands from the police, I kept cycling until they chased me. Looking suspicious, they searched me against a wall daily. Drifting from one day to another, there was not a whole lot to do.

The hostel was on the main road for all the busses that headed straight to Chris's house. Feeling bored, I went up to see him for a few hours. On the way back, I caught the 113 because it went past Louise's crescent. My life was never the same after what happened. The bus approached her stop. To my absolute amazement, she got on! Beating like a drum, my heart pounded like the very first time we met. Looking towards the road, it was best to not say anything. After paying, she sat near the back. What a bad idea taking that bus route; or maybe it was fate. A moment later I accepted her actions and took a deep breath. Sitting separately on the bus without acknowledging each other, was like the time before we started talking. The bus stopped near town when she stood up to get off. She whispered in my left ear, causing me to jump out of my skin!

"I still love you..."

Taking a deep gulp looking at the floor as she said it, she jumped off. I quickly followed behind her before the bus drove off.

"Louise, wait."

"I can't stop, I have to be at a tribunal."

"Can I walk with you?"

"Yeah, if you want."

Three months had passed, when my heart was starting to physically hurt.

"I miss you so much Louise, it's killing me."

"I miss you too, but we just can't be together anymore. You don't have anywhere to live, and my family won't let me see you."

The walk was only half a mile. The subject changed to something happier for one last time. I knew once we arrived, it would be the last time we would ever see each other.

"Can I hold your hand for one last time, I cheekily asked."

Smiling back at me, she said yes. Hand in hand, her touch drained away any pain. It was sad how everything turned out, but those few minutes made up for every fight and argument we ever had. I cherished that walk before reaching a red fence. She turned to give me a hug goodbye.

"Louise, kiss me one last time like you did when we first met."

Slowly pulling her head back brushing her sweet blonde hair against my cheek, we kissed with swirling tongues on the corner of Geoffrey street like we were the only two people on the planet. Opening my eyes, she was gone forever. My arms fell to my side for one last time. The months that followed became unbearable. Seeing a doctor was pointless; all the stitches in the world couldn't sew my heart back together.

Drinking every day in my room away from the staff, two new lads had moved onto my floor. One of them had attended my first high school the year below. Everyone knew him for being gay. The top floor was narrow, and we had to share the same lounge, making it hard to avoid him. He seemed harmless enough though. One weekend, a few of us decided to get together for a drink, once we sneaked alcohol past the staff. Buying half a litre of Brandy, the gay lad kindly bought it just for me. Being too young to sense any agenda that someone may have, it didn't occur to me why he spent £15 on me. The four of us had a laugh getting totally wasted without the staff even noticing. Drinking the whole bottle to myself from the pain inside, I was utterly wasted by midnight. Sat on the sofa, I must have passed out from drinking too much shortly after my housemates went back to their rooms. The next time I gained consciousness, I was lying in bed on my back looking up at the ceiling. My head felt like a boulder, leaving me unable to lift it up. My arms and legs became unresponsive. Looking down towards my feet, I could see the

gay lad in my room at the end of my bed. The dirty fucking bastard was performing oral sex on me. His real plan was abruptly revealed. With my arms by my side, it was impossible to move my hands towards my chest. From the neck down I was paralysed. Not knowing if I had been spiked, or just very drunk, I was horrified at what he was doing. I mumbled to him to stop. He laughed as if it was a joke telling me its OK. Getting his dick out, he started to play with himself at the same time. Lying helpless, there was nothing I could do. The thought of being raped entered my mind, but he never did. He left the room at some point after slipping back into unconsciousness. The next morning, I woke up in the same position with my pants back around my waist. An image of what happened quickly popped into my head. Was it a nightmare, I wondered? Having such a bad hangover, I knew it wasn't a bad dream. The first thing I did was get in the shower. Being straight, my body felt filthy. For twenty minutes, I sat on the shower floor curled in a bowl with shock. That was the most vulnerable feeling I ever experienced. It wasn't easy to talk about it, but I told the other lad that lived next to me, that same day.

"Mate, you have to go to the police and tell them."

"I can't. Do you know how embarrassing that will be, once the kind of people I know find out? My brother already calls me a puff and a faggot in front of his friends. I'd never hear the last of it if this went public."

Later that day, two men in suits called me into an empty room by the staff room. I freaked out thinking I had done something wrong.

"Hello Joseph, we're CID officers from the police station. Don't worry, you are not in any trouble. We are here about a complaint made by a friend of yours. We believe you were sexually assaulted late last night, is that true?"

Jesus Christ, I told him not to call the police. For the next half hour, I explained exactly what happened. He was arrested that night, losing his place at the hostel. A few days later I dropped the charges. My old friends practically lived in the Magistrates court. There was no way on earth I was taking the stand against him. Like Steven Wilding, he denied everything. My life and reputation would never be the same. Not to mention being classed as a grass. Being a snitch where I'm from was like telling a Muslim to burn the Quran. The matter would be dealt with out of court once I caught him, with the knife I started to carry.

No matter what I did, evil always found a way to attack me. Swinging blindly in the dark, spirits could not always be fought off with bare hands. It was time to arm myself before the hunter became the hunted. Truth is, I'd been hunted all my life.

Ending up in a temporary relationship with the two girls from the hostel, I wanted to forget the dirty feeling after being assaulted. Up to now, the year had been awful. A new Halloween movie had come out at the cinema, which was probably not the best time for any more bad influence. Not missing the chance to watch my favourite franchise, I took one of my girlfriends on a date. Too much bad was happening. It was time to go out for once. Not remember the last time I went out; my mood was positive. After buying some popcorn, we sat down near the back. John Carpenter's Halloween theme kicked in as two lads walked past us looking for a seat. Kirsty and I looked at each other in disbelief. The bastard that assaulted me walked right past me with his boyfriend and sat down. Blood boiled from inside me throughout the movie. Every time Michael Myers killed a victim, I envisioned doing the same.

"Calm down, don't let them get to you Joseph."

"Calm down? I want to kill him."

Half of the movie I spent staring at the back of his head, planning what to do outside. He was lucky I didn't have a knife on me. Films had such a significant influence on my mental state, ever since I was a child. It was an escape for me, to imagine being someone else. To bump into him with a knife, while watching Halloween at the same time, would have ended with me approaching him from behind, and stabbing him to death in his seat. After the movie finished, we stayed in our place to let him know we were there. Once

we got outside, they were both sat on the metal railing around the side of the cinema. Getting closer to him, he knew what I was going to do before I did it. Leaning his head to the right, my left punch flew over the top of him. All three of them shouted for me to stop while I lashed out. His six-foot-tall boyfriend tried to stop me, so I started to swing for him. Too tall for me to hit him, couples laughed at the fact that two lads bigger were running away to avoid my punches. The cowards ran off towards the docks begging for me to stop. He didn't know how lucky he was that night. Neither did I. From the way things were going, prison was almost inevitable.

After gradually getting kicked out of my hostel for breaking the house rules, a new associate from around the corner offered to let me move into his new flat. Knowing him as a getaway driver for one of the brother's that maliciously attacked the group of Muslim kids, he seemed OK. The reason they kicked me out of the hostel was because I got caught in one of the girl's rooms. I'd gotten away with it for months. Sending one of the lads to distract the staff, he asked them to open the locked freezer downstairs. Due to the number of sticky-fingered thieves, the freezer had to be locked at all times. Once downstairs, I ran from the top floor into one of the girl's rooms for the night. It all came to an end when the staff noticed how quiet I became, which was not like me at all. Thinking I could trust my new associate, I

moved all my stuff into his empty flat. PlayStation 2, a TV and other valuable things I had built up that year, had all been stolen. He walked away from his new flat just to rob me. Even I knew there was no honour amongst thieves. By then, my anger was through the fucking roof! I felt like a buffalo surrounded by hyenas. Each time my back was turned, some twat was taking advantage of me. Later that night, I drank half a bottle of vodka with the plan to cause as much destruction as possible. Armed with a metal bar, I kicked the door down to look for the bastard that just robbed me. Knowing he was long gone, I smashed every one of his windows from the inside. Being so cunning, I could see flashing police lights bounce off a wall as they approached. Throwing the metal bar into the long grass, I stood opposite the flat inconspicuously as a spectator. The police ran straight past me to search inside, leaving the police car unattended. An idea to jump in and drive off had entered my mind. Running towards the police car, I took a sharp right deciding to leave it. My next stop was the hostel I'd just left. Knocking on the big green door, the first person to answer was about to be on the receiving end of my fury. It was Kirsty that answered. For no reason, I dragged her outside against the staff room window. Out of pure rage, I tried to push her head through the window. Resisting me the best she could, I dragged her to the front door. Now on top of her, I grabbed her hair, bouncing her head off the floor. Completely out of control, Brian, my favourite staff member had to strangle me to get me off. That was the last thing I remembered. The

following morning, I woke up in some random girl's bed in the same hostel Chris lived in with his pregnant girlfriend. Within seconds of sitting up to look out of the window, a copper was walking up the street. He arrested me for the path of destruction. Apparently, I caused havoc in town after attacking Kirsty. Guilt stayed with me for what I did to her. With no excuses or condoning what I did, seventeen years of shite lead to that one night of destruction. It was fortunate I didn't kill anyone. Everyone was my enemy out for their own agenda. It was dog-eat-dog. Becoming paranoid from weed, my mum tormenting me for fun, and the pressure to survive, I found myself at boiling point. With no reasoning or understanding of what was happening to me, weeks later on a Saturday night, I walked into town towards drunk revellers with an eight-inch kitchen knife down my pants. Two drunken men sat on a bench eating chips. It was busy with people everywhere.

"What the fuck are you looking at?"

"Nothing mate, we're just sitting here."

Lifting my jacket up, I showed him the knife down my pants.

"I'll fucking stab you ya prick, what the fuck are you looking at?"

Lifting their hands up in the air, pleading with me, I felt a sense of control over my life again instead of being walked on. The thought of anyone trying to take advantage enraged me. No one will ever fuck with me again. That night was

about making a clear statement. My mum didn't get away with it, and neither will anyone else. Inside I was bleeding to death from my heart, becoming something I'm not; a bad person. My complexion reflected that of my mum and dad more and more. Maybe going with the flow was not such a good idea.

After failing to attend court for my path of destruction, a warrant was out for my arrest. One of my long-serving friends off the estate was up in crown court for carjacking a Mercedes with another lad, then taking police chase all the way to Scotland in a six-hour pursuit. I say, friend, because he had good parents, and the whole crime was down to another idiot. We shared the same fate getting into trouble, due to unfortunate circumstances. Place us both in a good environment from birth, and you can guarantee we would turn out good. People like him and me were the last ones to take part in crime. Coming up to eighteen, the rest of the lads began to sell drugs, moving up to armed robbery. What they wanted, they took. Being betrayed by his friend like I was, there was only a selected few with principles. He got eighteen months in prison. Down in manpower by over seventy percent, most of my estate was in jail. Talking to him down in the cells with his mum, I told him I'm coming with him. He laughed knowing what a crazy bastard I was. Two days later, I approached a copper in town to check if I had a warrant; which obviously I did. Standing before a judge the

following day, I asked him to refuse bail, and to send me to prison. He looked extremely baffled.

"In my twenty years or so as a judge, I've never known anyone to ask me to send them to jail. I don't know if you are insulting me, but your bail is denied until the next hearing."

That was the smartest thing I ever did. Unless I was under the influence of substances, any decisions I made were calculated. Making such a move solved three problems. The first was to get off the streets away from all the bad shit. The second was to avoid homelessness, and the third was to be with my friends. On the streets alone I had nobody. My life was safer in prison with a gang I had grown up with. At least I knew they had my back. It was also to sort my head out before I killed myself, or someone else. How the fuck it got to this point in the first place, was beyond me. Thinking I had control of my life, or that I was different than the rest seemed to be a mistake. Somehow I got caught up. They took me to a cell before my taxi arrived; the sweatbox.

Sat in the back of the prison van, an almighty excitement came over me. Maybe I was crazy like my dad after all. Each cubicle was about two and a half feet wide. Slapping my index finger against my thumb like a Rasta, I squealed up and down in my seat like a monkey in a fruit shop. The trick to surviving a situation is to become the situation. If someone shows fear, they will get eaten alive. If you can't

beat them, join them. The lad across from me looked in disbelief.

"Why are you so excited." He shouted

"It's my first time. Where are we going?"

"To HMP Lancaster farms."

I couldn't wait to see the look on my friends face when I walked in. Being the last person to pop my cherry, in terms of going to prison, it showed how well I did. Going to prison at seventeen was too old. Knowing what we were all capable of, I knew before arriving at that jail that nobody had seen the likes of us. We were the original circus.

"Hurry, hurry, hurry, step right up to the greatest show in town. The longest running freak show of all time. We have fighters. We have perverts. We have drug runners. We have murderers, and we have terrorisers. You name it, the circus has it. We also have, you named it, clowns. Lots and lots and lots of clowns. So, let's show this terrific audience the best the circus has to offer."

After being stripped searched, with my dignity going out the window a long time ago, I was clothed in grey jogging gear. Entering as new fish on my new wing, a large room stood before me full of people surrounded by cells. This is a prison? I should have come here years ago. Some lads were using the phones. Some lads played pool. There was even a row of televisions connected to Xbox's. Looking for my friend on all

the chairs by the front, I spotted him. He was watching a TV the size of a cinema screen. Am I even in the right place? I wondered. Who said crime doesn't pay? It certainly rewards. If I knew it was this good, without ambitions to go to America, I'd have done all sorts of crime. To think I'd slept on concrete floors, starved every day of the week, watched violence and nearly froze to death in the snow. What a joke. The only thing missing was a swimming pool with fine women around it. Still, I was adamant to at least try and stay on the right path. Looking at my friend, he sat in the middle of thirty empty chairs with his arms crossed. Letting him stew for a second before approaching, he looked really fed up.

"Oi you," I shouted with a smile on my face.

Once he clocked me, the look on his face was like a child on Christmas day. He jumped up like a spring chicken.

"Oh my gosh, you mad bastard. When you said you were coming, I didn't think you meant it."

"Yeah well, I'm a man of my word. Where's the rest of the lads?"

"Some have been shipped out. Were expected to get more soon. We have a few allies though. You see that big black guy three times bigger than everyone else serving food? Well, he's with us. On this wing its full of Manchester lads, and Scousers. If it kicks off, we side with the Manchester lads."

"Sound, just let me settle in my cell and I'll catch you up later. I'm wearing an extra pair of socks to shove a pool ball in if it kicks off."

It was comforting being apart of something. We knew each other's strengths and weaknesses. Growing up as kids, we stuck together through thick and thin. Parents live a lie hiding the truth from us, so how can we open up to tell them anything about what we already know? Looking at the faces in that prison, I didn't see any criminals; I saw lost teenagers crying out for attention. When friendships become a brotherhood, you will do anything to protect each other. They needed me as much as I needed them.

My wing was called Coniston 1. On arrival, they gave me a pouch of tobacco to smoke, but I didn't smoke. I had my own cell with a television, bed, toilet, and a radiator pipe that ran straight through. The next morning, I grabbed some breakfast, then sat on one of the tables with my crew meeting new associates. One lad I met, that was in there for selling heroin, was offering some sleeping tablets for my pouch of tobacco. Not caring for the tablets much, or if it was even a good deal, I accepted his offer. Maybe I could sell my tablets for something sugary. Finishing my food, I walked into my cell to get it for him.

"This doesn't look right, why do I have two pouches?"

"Giving the pouches to the lad for a couple of tablets, it soon dawned on me that I had walked into the wrong cell. All looking identical, I had walked in the one next to me, who happens to be a new lad like me. Walking next door into my actual cell, I shut the door before anyone noticed. Thirty minutes later, two screws marched in my cell.

"Stand up now. What the fucking hell do you think you are doing stealing from someone on your first day? Do you think you are a tough guy? Do you think you can act like that in this prison? We have you on CCTV. Where's his tobacco?"

"I gave it to another lad because I don't smoke. I walked into the wrong cell by accident."

"Who is he."

"I don't know, someone with blonde wavy hair."

"Less than 24 hours and you're in shit already. Stay in this cell, and don't come out for two weeks. You're on lockdown. We're taking your TV as well."

"But it was an accident, I swear."

Not believing a word from a presumed criminal, once again I was in deep water. The guards took the tobacco from the lad, to return it back to my neighbour. Now I had my original pouch in my top draw, a fist full of sleeping tablets, and some very pissed off heroin dealer thinking he just got scammed. What could possibly get worse in my life?

That was the slowest two weeks ever, but at least I wasn't hungry. During meal times, some lads would shout towards my door during my lockdown.

"Kane, you're going to get your head smashed in."

On top of the threats, my good friend was shipped out the next day to HMP Durham to serve his sentence. His luck didn't improve either. They placed him in a cell with no windows. That must have driven him mad. In fear of any reprisals, I had two weeks to prepare myself. All I could do was sit-ups and press-ups. I had more than a few lads for support, but that didn't enter my mind. They were in my world, and they didn't want to get trapped in my head with my intentions. If I had to cross that line, I'd cross it fully. They might be ready for a fight, but I was prepared for extreme violence. After two weeks of talking to myself, I was ready to cut someone's fucking head off. Jumping up and down behind my door with clenched fist, the guard came to release me. As soon as it opened, I marched out trying to make eye contact with everyone; forget eating. Walking past the same voices that threatened me, not one of them looked in my direction. Bunch of wimps, the lot of them. Behind every inmate, where failed parents. It should be them in prison, not us.

Appreciating my television back, I looked forward to 6pm. Every single day without fail, three ducks walked below my window. Opening just a tiny bit, they quacked below me in

clear sight. Not long after having my tea, I saved some food for them. They seemed to be a family. None of my family was ever there for me. No one even knew I was in prison. I believe it was God stopping by, to bring a message of hope. Time dragged, but it was good to clear my head. Those ducks helped my recovery. Thinking about what I said to the judge, it was the right move. Inside that secure prison, no one could get to me, or hurt me anymore. Becoming withdrawn from the general population, I decided to spend most of my time locked up. The peace and quiet was brilliant. No worries awaited me like my mum banging on my door or kicking me out. No responsibilities or expectations could disturb my sleep. Sat on the warm radiator at tea time, I watched the news while eating my food. I felt right at home. One night time I heard a familiar voice shouting for some information, but no other inmates responded. He sounded like another good friend of mine from back home.

"Oi you shouting, is that Lee?"

"Yeah, who's that?"

"Haaa, I thought it was you. It's me, Kane."

"Go on lad, what are you doing here?"

Lee was an all-round criminal but mainly dabbled in car theft, shoplifting, or smoking weed. It made me laugh to know he was inside. He spent his life in prison. The next day at dinner time, I joined him to hear his stories of how he started riots in that prison, along with another crazy kid from

back home. Whatever I wanted, he arranged. Apart from taking over one of the Xbox's, I was pretty content being alone in my little world.

Once I left prison, the courts gave me a fine after repaying more than my debt to society. My friends went on their path, while I tried to figure out my own. There had to be a reason behind the mask of doubt. It wasn't possible to suffer without eventually finding my purpose. I stayed at my mum's until the council placed me into another hostel. The same routine I had with schools began to show. All I ever wanted was to go home to a loving mum and dad, with some food on the table, proud of me for working hard at college. It's not much, just the basics; I can figure the rest out myself. Far from happening, I knew what time it was. The question was, when does this crazy life end?

Being over sixteen, doors opened for me, closing some behind. I had the option of going into care when I young, but from the stories I heard, I took my chances on the street. Reporting my mum for everything she had done came to mind. She wasn't worth it. I wasn't angry, she just broke my heart. My second hostel, fortunate to get in was made up of over thirty flats. My one-bedroom flat was on the top floor, in the very corner of the building. Most, if not everyone was homeless or screwed up in some form or another. The staff had more of a hands-on approach. It was just another zoo

with human tamers. The tenants were secure with twenty-four-hour support. The only benefit, was for everyone to do what the fuck they wanted. It was worse than prison. Everyone sold and took drugs, while the staff protected them with the police, and two secure doors at the front. Unless you had a fob, you couldn't get in. Visitors had to sign in, producing ID. If it were located in the middle of nowhere, everyone would benefit. How was anyone meant to fix their life, when the problem lives next door?

The flat across from me lived a guy called Antony. He was a nice quiet lad. Quiet in the sense that he kept to himself. All day he would blast his music, ignoring any calls from the staff on his intercom. Behind his closed door, was a one-man party for himself to shovel as much amphetamine down his neck as possible. Next door to me was a couple that always had sex. I'm pretty sure that's what made them homeless in the first place, but who would admit such a thing. The couple below me with two kids enjoyed a good party. They blasted three songs over and over, before fighting in the pit, also known as their living room. Another family similar to them had the biggest flat on the bottom floor. The butch-looking-lesbian was a baby machine to feed her habits. Having over four kids, they were the scummiest of them all; real bad people to say the least. Also on the ground floor was a man called Brian. In his fifties, Brian was a heavy drinker. He owned an allotment, surprisingly coming home with

shitloads of cash every day. His flat was filled to the rafters with stuff from his previous home. The staff allowed him to keep his pet snakes, just as long as they didn't escape. A snake on the loose in that building would have done wonders. He offered me £40 a week to clean his bathroom, which was a big help. I had to clean a toilet full of shit, and a bath you wouldn't dream of soaking in, but I didn't care as long as I had money in my pocket. Two doors away, a friend of mine had moved in. His life was like mine, but instead of his mum being an alcoholic, she was a speed freak. Both of us harassed Brian to see what money we could get out of him. We roamed around from flat to flat, watching all the crazy shit like it was a slideshow. Knowing more about myself coming up to eighteen, I enjoyed watching people's lives like a spectator. Always around different people, it was them that created footprints, and not me. My time was enjoyed talking to the staff by the entrance. An advantage to that was listening to other people's problems. Everyone had a story to tell.

Time in that hostel was a good buzz for most of it. Still smoking weed, and vast amounts of it, my friend introduced me to ecstasy with his group of friends. Always cautious about everything I do, I took small amounts to start with. What a fucking rush! I felt impervious to any afflictions. Wow, what a feeling. My friend took me to his mums one night to get some amphetamine. Only using the good stuff,

she had the yellow paste that was strong. As well as supplying her son, I thought I'd try some as well during my season experimenting drugs. The outcome ended in disaster for most, so my experiments were short lived. There was no way on earth I'm ending up like these scumbags. After dropping bombs with his mum (amphetamine wrapped in a rizla paper) the effect was not the same as ecstasy, but still pretty good. His eccentric hippy-looking mother gave me a small bag with some paste inside. Later going back to my flat, I was off my tits. The fun ended on the second day when I had not eaten or slept. The drug seemed like it was never going to wear off. Suddenly I collapsed on the floor. Still conscience, I looked up towards my door. A big red button on the intercom looked at me and winked. Feeling like I was about to die, I army crawled slowly towards the red button. Nearly completely incapacitated, somehow my arm reached up to press the button. Moments later, the staff answered the buzzer.

"Help me... Ring an ambulance."

The fault was all mine of course. Paramedics came to rescue me. They carried me by my arms to the elevator, then took me to hospital. An ambulance bed couldn't reach the top floor. Sat in a waiting room for over an hour, the drug finally wore off, so I signed myself out. That was it for me as far as drugs went. Even cannabis had to come to an end sooner or later. Weed wasn't doing my mental state any favours. I

stayed away from that friend because there was a new girl that had caught my eye.

On the floor below, I had met a mixed-race girl that looked pretty cute. She had a big smile that made me smile. In desperate need of some attention, I invited her up to my flat one night for a chat. Coming up to mine in her PJ's, we got on really well. She would never replace Louise, and I had some making up to do after what I did to Kirsty. Her family knew my stepfamily, so we already had something in common. Before long, romance blossomed, and we entered a relationship together. The sex was great, keeping me away from bad influences. She fell in love with me, and I had a lot of feelings for her, but for some reason, Louise was the love of my life. She stained me from loving anyone else. It had to be from the fact that she was my first love, and the impact she had on me. We continued to be happy though. Once again, I had landed on my feet. Being alone in such an environment was damaging to anyone. It could have been worse if I had met some scum bag.

Sadly, it was no fairy tale in that place. Some horrific things happened. The night I was taking amphetamine with my friend's mum, a US soldier was visiting his younger brother Adam at the opposite end of the hostel. The war in Iraq had not long started, with his brother completing his first tour. Inside the hostel, we had Muslim women with children, close

to Adams flat. His brother was drinking all night before deciding to call it a night by going home. Walking out of Adams flat, he walked down the long corridors, with pastel orange walls. On the corridor playing, was a two-year-old Muslim boy. Returning from my friend's mums, the whole building was surrounded by police. When I eventually got inside, I found out what had happened. Adams brother had picked up the child, thrown him against the wall, and then slam-dunked him on the floor like a basketball. In a moment of madness after his tour in Iraq, he was imprisoned for attempted murder. Fortunately, the child survived with his Army career was over. Not joining the Army seemed like a positive for me. Going to war would have really screwed up my head. It still didn't stop me from trying. Maybe it wasn't such a good idea anymore. Screaming soldiers in the face of an already broken person, then giving me a gun, was not a good idea.

Nearly every one of my bad situations seems to bring something good out of it, or so I thought. Stood near the reception desk swan-necking conversations, a young couple were arguing with each other. In a pram, they had a two-year-old son with blonde hair in the shape of a mushroom and blue eyes. He looked like me when I was his age. Linda and Marc came from Liverpool. Drug dealers threatened their life, so they came to Preston to escape. They only smoked cannabis. The threat had no weight to it, but having

a child wasn't worth the risk. Linda seemed very nice. She was a big girl with blonde hair, two years older than me and reminded me of someone. Marc had a shaved head and couldn't keep still, acting paranoid all the time. Befriending them, Linda told me how she was suffering from depression after her newborn had died. Showing me photos of the grave, it must have been hard on her. I didn't really like Marc, he wasn't very supportive and seemed very odd. I visited their flat a few times to talk to them. Linda became my best friend. The reason I had got so involved with them, was because Linda had formed a relationship with another lad in the hostel. Steven on the ground floor was a real weasel. Thinking he was Eminem, he rapped in his flat all day. Already in a relationship myself, Linda and I could have had something special if things were different. Never getting mixed up with current relationships, she needed a friend. Steven couldn't give Linda what she wanted. He was a loser. The love triangle got complicated with Linda backwards and forwards to each flat. All I could see was a desperate lad coming between a family that needed support. She was one of the nicest girls I'd ever spoken to. We confided in each other. It felt like God had sent me an angel. Stood in Marc and Linda's flat seeing if I could help, Ste was at the front door talking shit, taking advantage of a vulnerable girl. Being the one that opened the door, he stood close to me resting his smug face against the door frame. Where I came from, he was known as a muppet. Seeing a tear roll down my best friend's face, I rested my left foot keeping the door open. I

246

punched the prick straight in his jaw, bouncing his head off the door frame to break the love triangle up. Jumping backwards, he ran off down the corridor with me behind him. For three solid days, I chased that weasel around the whole building.

"Go on Joseph!"

People cheered me on during one of our laps around the long building. After a week, I caught him on my bike over a mile away from the hostel. We bumped into each on the street by accident. Before he had time to think, I jumped off my bike and punched him in the face a few times. Not known for fighting, my hatred for cowards was beginning to grow. I tried being a coward, and it's a shitty thing to do with no honour. Out of nowhere, morals, principles and values suddenly mattered. That was hard to digest given my environment.

When the dust settled weeks later, Linda approached me out on the front wall with a smile.

"How are you doing sweetheart?"

"Good thanks. I need to talk to you, Joseph."

"Of course."

"Marc has asked me to move to Manchester with him for a fresh start."

"If you want to get away from these two, you can come and live with me at my mums. I don't care what she thinks."

"I appreciate that, but I don't know what to do."

"You should go for it. Maybe it will turn out to be a good thing."

Steven was ruining her relationship with Marc and her son. A fresh start could improve their life. Jumping off the wall, I wrapped my arms around her black and white checkered coat and gave her a big squeeze. Ste and Marc kept peeping through the window, jealous how close we were. The following few days, they took off on their new adventure. Hostels were no place for families.

Brian from downstairs had been attacked by some idiot that went to my school. His face was black and blue, barely able to open his eyes. You don't even have to do anything wrong to be attacked, it just happens. Violence was fun for some people. Having been on a waiting list for a flat, my time in the fun house was coming to an end, to make way for more screwed up people. Up on the top floor, I was chilling in a woman's flat one night with a crazy bitch, that coincidently shared my mum's name. She's OK to be around, as long as no one gets on her bad side. Much older than me, she lived with a young daughter. That night with her friend and sister coming around, we all had a laugh. Her sister was stunning, just a bit younger than me. She had everything to live for.

What I didn't know was that they had a bad childhood. When Angie's sister went to the toilet, she started whispering to us on the sofa.

"Watch her, keep your eye on her in that bathroom."

"What do you mean."

"she self-harms."

"we have to hide any knives from her."

A minute later she came out of the bathroom. The night went well after a few drinks. Being everyone's friend, I was up and down like a yo-yo. After an hour, her sister went to the bathroom again. On our own vibe, we had all been distracted to how long she had been in the bathroom.

"Where she gone now?"

"I don't know. The bathroom I think."

With Angie running to the door, nothing could prepare us for what happened next. The second that bathroom door opened, something from a horror movie was inside. Rushing to the bathroom, it looked like a slaughterhouse. There was blood everywhere. Her sister didn't just do a few scratches like me, she sliced as deep as possible with the sharpest knife. Slumped on the floor, this beautiful young girl was bleeding to death.

"Joseph, take the knife quick."

Going faint from my own blood, I put the kitchen knife in a sink full of water. Apparently, she got the blade from the

kitchen the second she arrived. The shiny metal at the bottom of the water reflected my red face through the blood. Wrenching my guts up in the sink, I was no good to anyone. Angie's friend called an ambulance, while she tried to stem the bleeding. That was the most horrifying thing I'd ever seen, and I've seen some pretty fucked up shit. Blood was everywhere. Thank god the paramedics came to take her away. She somehow survived that night. I don't know what came of them after that. When I leave that place, I have no interest to keep in touch with anyone.

My intercom bleeped in my flat.

"Do you want to come down Joseph, I've got a flat for you."

Walking downstairs anxiously, she laid it down to me. After my last flat, I knew I wasn't ready. Overstaying my welcome, I had to leave. We arrived at a three-storey block of flats, exactly the same as the ones I had stayed in when my mum kicked me out in the snow. The ground floor flat was the one we viewed. It was next door to a smack-head woman that had just left the hostel before me. She had no legs from injecting heroin. You would expect her to stop using drugs, not carry on. It was a shithole. My door was made out of wood and glass. Anyone could kick it in. With the prospect of living next to heroin users, I didn't have a choice. Turning it down went against me. Not having any furniture, Jane found a house full of stuff. A family had split up leaving absolutely everything. Leaving the baby toys, I took the bed, sofa, fridge

and other useful items. My flat had no carpet, single glazed windows and dodgy doors. Having no cooker, I lived off takeaways in a freezing cold flat. To me, it was worse than death. To top things off, there were some bad lads across from me that I knew. One lad was cool, the rest were pure bad.

Once I moved out to somewhere I didn't want to be, I returned to my hostel for any letters. On my way back, I bumped into Antony who tormented everyone with music.

"Have you heard what happened?"

"no, what?"

"Do know Linda that moved out?"

"Course I know Linda."

"She got murdered in Manchester. Her boyfriend murdered her in some woods."

". . . . . . "

My legs melted like wax. I had to sit on the curb behind a takeaway from shock. I couldn't hear a word of what Antony said after that. He walked away. What had I done? I sent my best friend to her own death. Walking into my hostel, the staff confirmed it. Returning home, I turned on the TV for

the six o'clock news. Linda's sweet face appeared on the screen.

"We bring sad news tonight, a nineteen-year-old mother was murdered in Manchester, close to woods. The police encourage anyone to come forward for any information. Tributes have been paid out to the young mum, who leaves behind a two-year-old son."

After listening to what happened, I cringed in tears screaming. The pain inside was unbearable. Marc denied it was him. Two weeks later he came on the news. He was caught by a single spec of blood on their son's shoes, forcing him to admit it. Paranoid that she was going to leave him, he battered her in the woods in front of their son. When she was on the floor, he smashed her head in with a rock. For no reason other than pure evil, he rammed a tree branch down her throat before engraving his initials into a tree. All I could picture was her beautiful hair in the mud. Linda came to me before anyone else, in faith to guide her and I let her down. For all the stupid shit I did, my friend was gone forever and its all my fault. Its something I will always feel responsible for. Nineteen was too young. I was sick with anguish. Marc was found guilty, getting a life sentence. Fifteen years was not long enough for killing Linda. His bizarre face came on the news with a really long beard. His piercing eyes were wide open. I wanted to kill him. Thoughts came over me about committing a serious crime, to get on a category A wing, just to get at him. It made no difference. She was gone

forever, and there was nothing I could do about it. I couldn't face the funeral, so I stayed in Preston. The pain was too raw, and with no way to get to Liverpool, I missed it. A part of me couldn't admit it, leaving me indenial. My heart wept for her poor son that was now with Linda's family. Marc was initially from Burnley, which said it all. I hated Burnley, and I hated Marc. Nothing could give me answers or heal the pain after losing her. Her warm body in my arms will be forever etched in time. It will take a long time before I can say goodbye. I loved her so much from the short amount of time we had. She can rest with her newborn baby in heaven. I knew she was an angel the first time I laid eyes on her.

Not long after, Antony hung himself. He owed drug dealers money. After beating him up already, with mental health problems from all the speed he was taking, I imagine he felt like there was no way out of his situation. My thoughts manifested sat in my lonely flat all the time. My life felt like an empty shell, waiting for something to crawl in and walk away. Trying to separate my chav life, to enter into mainstream normality was almost impossible. I hated how the lifestyle stripped any innocence. I wanted to be that kid again that sat on the wall all day, outside my mums in the sun. So much had changed. I couldn't go back. I'd come too far to turn back; the only way now was forward. I've had the pleasure of my loving grandparents, the joy of falling in love to the point of my soul detaching, and the chance to travel

the world before meeting an angel. There had to be a way forward. I just don't think I deserved it.

Hanging around with the losers on my front, they were different to the certain lads I knocked about with. Hoping to get away from criminals, I was right back in with a circle of idiots. Like cowards, they took advantage of poor situations, always trying to fight with someone weaker. One of them was on my level, the rest of the four were evil. Trying to quit smoking weed, I refused one of them from coming in my flat. He disrespected me the week before by kicking over a mop bucket on purpose, leaving me to clean up all the water. I even got arrested for one of them for possession of weed. He'd only just been released from the police station for another incident, so I did him a favour. Some good it did. My crew from back home were nothing like those scavengers. That night I got into bed in my freezing flat. There was no central heating. The building was ready to be knocked down. Climbing into three layers of bedding, seconds later I heard a loud bang. Someone was kicking my door in. Getting dressed was my first priority. Stood terrified in my dark bedroom, the noise fell silent. Just about to jump out my window, thoughts went through my head. "I'm not a pussy." Whatever is out there, I'll face it like I always. My grandad swam across a river to get away from bullies as a teenager; that's not happening to me. The next minute, the flat door upstairs was being kicked in. After the silence came, I walked out to head

to the next landing above me. Looking at the smashed door, a man behind the glass was waving a knife.

"When I get out, I'm going to fucking kill you."

"It wasn't me, I'm from the flat downstairs."

Not really listening to me, I walked down the stairs. Just as I did, the vultures arrived. It was the same group of idiots I'd been hanging around with. Pissed up, they came looking for trouble. The seven of them stood next to me, not saying much. Two of them had respect for me. The rest had no respect for anyone. I tried to blend in choosing what I said. In certain circumstances, a person has to say certain things if they don't want to be targeted. It was a skill I developed over the years. Being ninety-nine percent effective, it fell on deaf ears that night. One of them was the cousin of the two brothers that attacked the Muslim children. His presence concerned me. Not really knowing who I was, he punched me in the side of my face. It was the softest punch I'd ever felt. I planned to fall down to my knees as a sign of submission. That night I got it completely wrong. The moment I went down, they kicked me like a football. They kicked so hard that I ended up in the opposite corner. I faced the wall and covered my head with my hands, waiting for their legs to tire. My back took some horrendous blows from eight legs, one after the other. Surely my slender frame couldn't withstand such a beating. The first few kicks went with ease; my ribs held firm as I curled up tighter. After ten kicks I started seeing white flashes. I could feel my life slipping away. They

weren't even going for my head. if they didn't stop in the next ten kicks, I'm done for. I opened my eyes and braced for my death. Even with my eyes open, the flashes got brighter. Every flash, I started to see Linda. The dirty concrete in front of me was the last thing I was about to see before dying. Not feeling the pain anymore, they carried on with the flashes turning into a permanent white light. Not responding to any more kicks, Linda was stood before me in an empty white room. She was smiling but didn't speak. Her vision lasted, even without kicks. An empty silence was all I could hear. The place I was in had no emotion or physical feelings. Is this it? Am I dead? Is Linda here to greet me? No more kicks... No more shouting... No more flashes... Just an endless white...

Thank you for taking the time to read my story. We all have a story to tell whether it's good or bad. Writing this book was painful. However, the more I went over it, the more I came to terms with what happened. Some content was too evil to add, so I decided to leave it out. This book covers my life from the age of 4 to 17. At some point, I will write the second chapter of my life that will cover my age from 17 to 30.

Wanting to show off my beautiful friend, here is a link to the news story about Linda Neale. RIP Princess. You will never be forgotten x x x x x x

http://news.bbc.co.uk/1/hi/england/manchester/3205336.stm

I would appreciate it if you could give me a good review on Amazon, it really helps people find my book. Also, share to someone that might be interested in my story. Sharing is caring. Please follow my profile page on Amazon so that I can update you on any future work I create. As a new author, I plan on writing personal development books to help people.

GOD BLESS

Printed in Great Britain
by Amazon

38021359R00147